Ozana Giusca

Business Unlimited
Smarter Profits Faster

- Volume 7 -

Take that Giant Leap

101 Zero-Cost Tactics to Take Your Company to the Next Level

Amaze Yourself With What YOU Can Achieve Further!

Copyright © 2017 Ozana Giusca
All rights reserved.

ISBN-13: 978-1978361911
ISBN-10: 1978361912

To all the business owners and entrepreneurs I have worked with: thank you for entrusting me with growing your business.

To my team, who have put so much effort into building Tooliers, the high-end business growth tools and programs that are transforming businesses around the world, a big thank you for going through the ups and downs with me.

Thank you for helping me with this book. We wouldn't be here without your dedication and contribution!

I would like to name the Tooliers core team: Vali, Dragos, Sorana & Catalina. You are like family to me! I am so grateful you joined me in my journey!

Table of Contents

Foreword	V
Preface	VII
My Story	IX
Introduction	1
Bonus • Steady Growth - Systematize Your Business	**4**
Tactic #1 • Follow a System	5
Note: Tactics #2 - #86 are in Volumes 1-6	
Take that Giant Leap	**12**
Tactic #87 • Embrace Innovation	13
Tactic #88 • Learn from Startups	18
Tactic #89 • Create a Startup Environment	23
Tactic #90 • Follow Your Passion	27
Tactic #91 • Bring New Voices into Your Company	32
Tactic #92 • Bring in Experts	36
Tactic #93 • Bring the Person(s) You Need into Your Business Today	42
Tactic #94 • Fire the Person Holding You Back	46
Tactic #95 • Know TODAY. Anticipate TOMORROW	50
Tactic #96 • Identify Your Prospects' Needs Even Before They Do	57
Tactic #97 • Identify Your Clients' REAL Needs	60
Tactic #98 • Leverage Your Platform for Maximum Results	65
Tactic #99 • Expand Your Distribution Channels	68
Tactic #100 • Leverage with Technology	73
Tactic #101 • Constantly Look for New Ideas	76
Smart Business System™	**80**
Bonus • Love Letter	**92**
Love Letter Template	94
Love Letter Example	95
Glossary of Terms	**98**

Foreword

The world is changing so fast. These events are opportunities for those who grab them, and at the same time can negatively affect those who do not take action. Most small businesses find it harder to break through their current level. They reach a plateau and do not know what step to take next, or go beyond 'small' and lose the plot.

There is so much information available now about how to run a successful business, but the challenge is to find meaning within this information and to use it appropriately to optimize and grow your business. In my experience as a small business consultant, I have seen a lot of business owners who cannot simply and quickly explain what they do, let alone generate interest and sell their products or services. I also see that entrepreneurs have dreams and goals, yet 80% of their time is spent on things that have no link whatsoever with their objectives. If they do not focus on what is needed to achieve their goals, how can they get there?

If you are looking for a very hands-on approach to building your business from the ground up, Ozana has nailed it in *Business Unlimited*. What a purposeful read for anyone who is an entrepreneur or small business owner. As you continue on your business or career journey, you will face real challenges that may deter you from achieving your biggest goals. The tactics in this book will keep you on track and help you reach your goals in record time.

In our lives we have the opportunity to do it the hard way or to learn from what the experts do, and then do it better. Ozana has been trained by some of the best in the business, including business and marketing guru Jay Abraham. In this new book you will discover key observations and ingredients to create even more success in your life and business. The real-world examples, as well as the practical exercises at the end of each tactic, also ensure this is a user-friendly manual to reaching business success.

Foreword

In *Business Unlimited*, you will learn to see the bigger picture of your business as well as discover the importance of *systematically* improving it; that is, by prioritizing and focusing on those areas that most need improvement. You will learn to identify your best customers; let go of any customers who do not lift your business; learn from your competitors; and fulfil the core purpose of every business: providing *real value* to your customers. You will also discover how creating the right kind of partnerships will grow your business with little extra effort on your part. Business owners will find the tactics on closing sales and creating urgency especially valuable. You will also see how essential it is to build relationships both with your best customers and your team.

This book is also brutally honest about areas in which business owners tend to waste time and resources – and provides a wealth of best practices for time management; this includes a reminder to employ the time-saving advantages of certain technologies. You will also be encouraged to reflect and act upon your role as a leader and to go beyond merely managing your business to making sure it leads to the kind of life and lifestyle you desire. Aspects like personal branding, networking and being open to change are also discussed. Finally, you will clarify your vision in order to take your brand into the future and be left with a business that is dynamic and that constantly strives for – and achieves – improvement and growth.

The bottom line: if you are ready to increase your success rate today, take the time to read this mind-expanding book two to three times, and then implement the ideas that are shared here.

Bill Walsh

America's Small Business Expert

Website: billwalsh360.com

Preface

If you answer YES! to any of these statements, this book is for you.

- You have achieved some success with your business, but seem unable to grow it further.
- You are not satisfied with where your business is.
- You are not getting enough from your business (you are not getting enough recognition or enough money, or you have not succeeded in fully achieving your Objectives).
- Work is taking over your life and you have no time for family, relaxation, or travel.
- You are still struggling to make a living.
- You are bored with your work! You want something more challenging and fun.
- You are missing something, but you're not sure exactly what.
- There are some areas you do not understand (for example, finance) or you are passionate about your product, but you cannot sell it.
- You just want to be sure that you are on top of things and that your business is on the right track.
- You have some ideas for new businesses, but are not quite sure how to go about it.
- You want new challenges, but you need your current business to continue to run for various reasons (financial, community).
- Your turnover and/or profits have started decreasing.
- You can anticipate a disaster but you cannot tell what exactly is happening.
- Your best employees have started to leave.
- You have lost your biggest client.
- You seem to deliver good quality but your clients are still not prepared to pay what you'd like for your products.
- There has been a recent change in your company's industry or outside

environment and this has had a great impact on your business.
- You and your staff are working too hard and it is just not fair on any of you (especially given the results you achieve).
- You consider your company a victim of your crisis, a system, or something else.
- Your business has stopped serving the community.
- Your business is growing quickly and you are struggling to manage it. It is becoming too complex for you to run on your own.
- Your life is too stressful. There are just too many problems that need to be solved by you, the business owner.
- You and your co-owners have trouble running the business together.
- Your business has started experiencing problems or you foresee problems, but you don't know what to do about them.
- You have accumulated too much debt in your company and can no longer sustain it.
- You simply want to discover the latest strategies that Fortune 500 companies use for their success!

My Story

I want to take a few minutes to ask you the questions that are on every small business owner's mind:

- What is the REAL secret behind businesses that generate more profits while their owners are enjoying life and doing what they want, when they want?
- Can I get more customers to call us instead of *us* chasing *them*?
- How can I get a great team of committed employees to work hard so we grow the business together?
- Is there any way to feel happier with my business and really achieve what I set my mind to?
- Ultimately, how can I, a small business owner, entrepreneur or freelance expert, make a difference in the world?

I get asked these questions all the time and it's why I wrote this book. Via this book, the tools, programs, events we deliver, I provide the answers to these questions, and many more.

Before you dig in, let me tell you a little about myself…

In 2007 my life seemed perfect. I was a rising star, doing everything most people would love to do.

After attaining my MBA from Cass Business School, London in 2000, I worked in the City for a few years. In 2003, I set up my own consulting firm, where I advised on selling a few companies and raised hundreds of millions in bank finance for various projects.

While my business generated a decent income, I knew I was on my way to support other entrepreneurs help more people and make a bigger impact.

With a team of 12 consultants, I was living my dream. I could party, travel, wear my favorite brands…

My Story

I bought a flat, then another one, then an office for our company, a new car... until the financial crisis hit my business badly, as happened with thousands of businesses around the world.

All of a sudden money stopped flowing in. The banks withdrew from financing our transactions; those hundreds of thousands of dollars in success fees never arrived; and ongoing consulting projects got put on hold. No more new business meant no more cash.

Imagine: By January 2009, I had let most of my team go. For me, they were not just staff, they were *family*. And they were damn good at what they did.

With more than a million dollars in debt, I could no longer pay the bank. Many sleepless nights followed... I felt ashamed, convinced people would point a finger at me, accuse me of not paying my debts. I got scared thinking about a potential bad credit rating and that I might never be able to get a loan again.

I felt my reputation as an honest, trustworthy businessperson was ruined as I couldn't pay my debts.

I had no money coming in and was borrowing on a monthly basis to pay my two remaining staff members. I was driving to my father every weekend to get food for the week for me and my partner.

It seemed that every phone call I got, every email I received, brought more bad news.

Watch this: my phone service provider threatening to end my contract should I not pay my bills. Imagine trying to save a business without a phone connection or access to the internet!

That was it, I decided. *Enough!* I borrowed more money and paid for an event in London where 15 successful entrepreneurs shared their strategies on how they became profitable. I learned about online marketing, selling one-to-many via events and social media advertising. Most importantly I realized the need to be visible to the right audience.

How many of these tactics do you think I applied? None! Because I soon realized I was in the wrong business anyway. Yep, this was my biggest take-away from the conference. I realized there was nothing special about me or my business, nothing that would get clients to choose our services.

There were too many people doing the same thing, making it difficult to differentiate myself.

As I had all this cutting edge knowledge, I started applying it to the businesses of former clients, and friends. And *this* is how I started earning again…

It turned out my consulting business was not the only business lacking proper business knowledge! In fact, most small businesses lack such knowledge – they are usually set up based on an opportunity the founder sees, based on the founder's skills and abilities. Yet businesses are complex and no entrepreneur can know it all; certainly no one can handle everything.

I also discovered my special gift: being able to identify where a business is leaving money on the table and how they can double or even triple their profits by making a few important changes.

My skill became immediately obvious as I managed to achieve:

- **30% increase in Sales within a month** for a client in hospitality (hotel) and a **287% increase in their online bookings within three months.** Their occupancy rate was 10% when we started working together – now it's in excess of 50%.

- **8 Sales during the first workshop** for a weight loss solution – a full house event achieved within five days of promotion. In fact, we had to close the doors and leave people outside disappointed.

- **$40,000 in Sales generated for a book** that had been sitting idle on Amazon before

> *With the right tools YOU too can turn your business around*

we started working with the author/chiropractor.

- **15% increase in Sales** for the main distributor of promotional materials, who already had 50% market share.

Over the past three years, I have personally helped more than 100 companies achieve massive growth. Some companies increased Sales by 30% within the first month of working with us; others tripled their Sales within a year.

I put all the knowledge I gathered – and much more – into what is today known as **Business Lens™**, a toolkit to identify what business owners don't do well or enough of in their company. This is **a tool that reveals the naked truth about any business**. It measures, mathematically, the gap between your company and Best Practices. The bigger the gap, the more growth potential the company has. Plus, it shows business owners where they need to focus to maximize Sales and profits.

This was the start of Tooliers, the platform with Smart Business solutions for small enterprises to increase profitability and become leaders in their niche. We now have clients around the globe and what's most important is not that we are making money, but that we help those who need us and our tools to smarten their businesses and achieve bigger profits faster.

Above all, I am proud of having built something that lasts beyond me. I know people will benefit from my current activities even after I am no longer here.

What's really in it for me? Or you?

> When you focus on the right things in your business, you have the recipe to success

FREEDOM!

The freedom to do what I want, when I want; to live anywhere in the world… and most importantly to be ME!

> *So what does this have to do with you and your business?*

You too can have the FREEDOM you want!

And I guess this is one reason you are reading this – you know you can do more and you want to.

The economy changes rapidly these days. As a small business owner, it is easy to run your business as if lost in a dark forest, thinking only of *survival*. You might forget about the destination. You are most likely involved with paying the next bill, dealing with a crisis after your best employee has left, trying to make up for that lost customer, deciding what kind of paper to buy for the copy machine and many other activities that keep you 'busy' and working hard.

But do you work *smart*? What if there was **a better way to achieve those dreams** you had when you started your business?

One third of business owners **want to grow their businesses, but don't know how and where to start**. The rest would like to maintain their business. The reality, however, is that 80% of businesses fail in the first five years and 96% in the first 10 years (this according to Michael Gerber, author of The *E-Myth*).

These facts also inspired me to write this book. I want to help YOU, a business owner, to *enjoy* your entrepreneurship. I want to help driven entrepreneurs just like you to achieve the success you deserve.

Business Unlimited is a collection of Best Practices I have seen and learned during my 20-year career in professional services. I learned about these tactics from seminars, workshops, conferences and summits,

My Story

and I have tried and tested them on my business and on our clients' businesses. When you master the tactics that follow, you will be able to compete with multinational companies, with Fortune 500 companies, as their equal. Because you know what? They use exactly the same tactics you are about to discover.

This book is part of my mission to empower 1,000,000 entrepreneurs to change the world while they achieve their personal and professional objectives fast, with ease.

Happy reading and enjoy the transformation of your business!

Ozana

Your Smarter Profits Accelerator

P.S. If you are serious about growing your Sales and profits, raising your profile and helping way more people, I invite you to join any of my online or live Master Classes and bootcamps.

Visit My Events Page *(www.ozanagiusca.com/my-events)* to get the updated schedule of my events and register to those most suitable for you.

Why have I written this book?

I wrote this book because I believe YOU can achieve much more especially in today's economy, which is the best possible environment for driven entrepreneurs and small businesses to really take off and finally get to the next level, especially because of the Internet and technology developments.

I believe that small businesses are changing the world and making it a better place... provided they deploy the right systems. Thus, this book is about a systematic approach to business so you achieve your dreams and gain the respect you deserve.

Turning around my own company from the brink of bankruptcy in 2008 to a business selling on all continents was an incredible journey. Having been through 3 years with no sales (before Tooliers took off), I made every possible mistake. I also realised that business can be fun. So I made it my mission to empower 1,000,000 entrepreneurs to make a bigger impact, by proving them with full clarity on their business, and, of course, the right tools. Bottom line, I want to reduce the entrepreneurial struggle by encouraging small business owners and experts to first think strategically and then implement any tactic they consider. This way, they finally get results quickly with no stress or overwhelm.

This book is about sharing some of the lessons we've learnt so you build a profitable business and unleash your unlimited potential... **hence BUSINESS UNLIMITED**.

You hear me talk about Smart Business, which is the vehicle to get there... A Smart Business is flexible in approach, leverages what you have and know, and systematically attracts clients online so you scale and grow exponentially. This, of course, enables you, its founder and commander, to be anywhere you want, and not chained to your desk 16 hours per day.

My Story

Regardless of being early stage or a successful entrepreneur, if you are driven to achieve more, to create more value, to serve more people and improve their lives while you get what you want, then I would love to support you in your journey.

Let's change the world together!

Introduction

How to use this book

You don't have to start with Tactic 1, or to read this collection chronologically. Start with the tactic that feels the most interesting to you. Each tactic addresses a different Stage of a business. You may find one tactic more relevant than another. Read the relevant ones first and feel free to jump from one tactic to another.

You will see that each of the 101 Tactics concludes with a short exercise that will make it easy to apply the tactic to your business. If you are serious about growing your business, it is essential that you *decide how to apply* the tactic you have just read and *do the exercises* that follow. While doing the exercises, write down whatever comes to mind.

Don't get overwhelmed by all the information in this book. You don't have to use it all at once. However, you will be surprised by how much of this book applies to you and your business. Take the knowledge on board, and don't get desperate if you can't find a way of using it on the spot. The more you practice using these tactics, the more ideas you will get – in time you may even find ways to use those tactics you thought were not relevant to your business.

Revisit the book as your business Needs and Goals change. Reread certain tactics, or tackle new ones. This book may well become your 'Bible for a Smarter Business'.

The finer details

Definitions of all words or terms that appear in **bold and italics** or starting with Caps can be found in the Glossary of Terms.

I use **customer** as a generic term. In your industry, you may prefer the word client, visitor, guest, user, or patient, for example.

I use examples from **a range of industries**. Feel free to adapt and apply the tactics to your own business.

Throughout the book, I use **products** and **services** interchangeably. Note, however, that an **offering** is not the same as a product or service. For our purposes, an offering refers to the product or service combined with its price, packaging and positioning. So, product X as offering A is sold for $100 as a stand-alone product. Product X could also be packaged as offering B, which includes another item or addresses a different market or just has a different packaging, and sells for $200.

Example:

> Cashew nuts can be sold in large quantities (tons) to wholesalers, who then repackage the nuts in smaller quantities (say 1 kilogram) to be sold at the market. Those same cashew nuts can be sold in supermarkets in packs of 300 grams; these look more attractive and command a higher price. Or the cashew nuts can be sold per 100 grams in a high-end bar, for a premium price.
>
> The product is the same – cashew nuts – but with different packaging and/or positioning, it becomes a different offering and commands a different price.
>
> The target market could be the same or different. I could be buying a 1 kg pack at the market, but I could also buy the 300 gram packs in gas stations.

Introducing Tooliers®

Tooliers® (www.tooliers.com) is THE latform with high-end business growth solutions to empower entrepreneurs to build their SMART business so they increase profitability, reduce struggle and become leaders in their niche.

Business Lens™ is the digital mirror of your business. It shows you the naked truth about your business. It shows your unrealized growth potential.

Business Lens™ Diagnosis is the process of using Business Lens™ to perform a full analysis of your business, which identifies the areas that need more of your attention so you take your business to the next level.

Business Doctor is one of our growth programs, where we perform the Business Lens™ Diagnosis, and issue suggestions and recommendations for tactics and strategies to execute, so you grow your business immediately as well as long term.

Businesses don't grow unless people grow. You rock! By reading this book, you are enabling personal growth together with business growth!

Bonus:
Steady Growth -
Systematize Your Business

Follow a System

Focus your efforts exactly where they are required as your business grows

I have created the **Business Growth Focus Formula** (see below) because so often I see business owners focusing on the wrong things. You want to do what you like to do, or what you are best at and this is fine to a certain extent. But if you want to have a *highly successful business*, you need to approach it systematically, and change Focus according to which Stage your business is at. Focus doesn't mean you only work on a certain area of your business or that you do it all by yourself. It means you **concentrate your efforts on a particular area of your business at a particular time.** It also means that you learn more about that area. Of course, you can involve Experts and you can Delegate, as long as this area is where your mind is. Even if you outsource, you inevitably acquire more knowledge in that area.

> *Be disciplined and Focus on what you have to in order to reach your Objectives and fulfill your dreams*

The idea is simple: your Focus, as the owner of the business, moves from 'Sales' to 'Sources and Resources' to 'Systems', as your company grows. This is the **best business growth strategy**. Focusing on one part of the business does not mean that you *only* deal with that part. It means, say, that you allocate half of your time to it, while the other half is split between anything else you would normally deal with. Above all, you, as the business owner, must focus on what needs your Focus, even if it is not necessarily what you *like* doing.

Let's talk about each area of a business:

Business Growth Focus Formula

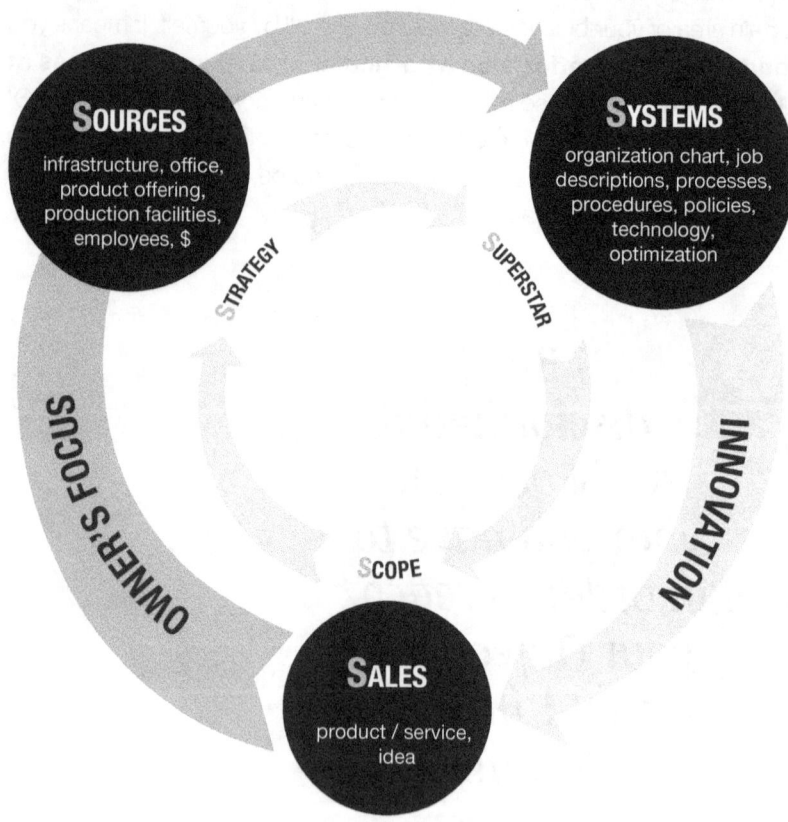

1. Focus on Sales

When you are at the beginning with your business, or when you launch a new product or open a new location. 'Sales' is split into two parts:

(i) selling your product or service;

(ii) selling your idea.

Selling your product or service is what you would generally understand as: giving your product / service to your customer in exchange for money (the price paid).

Selling your idea means getting people to buy into what you are doing. To share your dream, your vision and to get others excited about it. Selling your idea to current employees, potential employees, partners, suppliers, banks and any other person who is necessary to run the business smoothly, is as important as selling your product. You cannot create a business on your own. To achieve your Objectives, you need people around you. And those people don't join just because you think they should. It is tempting to believe they see and understand as you do, but they don't. You have to give them reasons to opt in, just as you give reasons to your customers to buy your product.

During this Stage, you have only a **Scope**. You know where you want to get to, but it is still flexible. You need the market reaction and partners' Feedback in order to ensure you have the right product, the right offering, both for your *customers* and for your business partners. The offering for the *customer* is a widely used concept: 'Buy this product for this price because it solves this problem in this way.' The offer for *business partners* sounds something like this: 'Bring customers to our business and you get x% from all the money they spend with us.' This is how you have to think of the Value proposition for your customers and your business partners. All parties have to win. And everything has to make sense and be clear from the outset.

2. Focus on Sources and Resources

Once your product or service sells by itself; in other words, when customers buy your product or service without you having to convince each of them individually. By 'Sources' I mean everything that enables you to deliver to your customer; that is, your overall infrastructure: production facility, office space, logistics, as well as your employees and money to buy raw materials and invest in further growth. No point selling if you can't deliver, right?

When you have gotten to this phase, **you have a Strategy in place.** Now that you know what and how you sell, and for how much, you can create Specific Objectives and a clear path to achieving them.

3 Focus on System

When you are confident that you have a product that sells and that you can deliver and satisfy your customer. By 'Systems', I mean organizational charts, job descriptions, processes, procedures, policies, IT system, and potentially CRM / ERP (software to help with planning and managing your Resources and your customers).

In this phase you **consolidate what you have**; you organize things internally and clean up your mess. By this Stage, you and your staff have tried various ways of producing and delivering Value and you now know who does what in your company, and how. It is therefore time to document everything that is happening in your company, to put order in place. This helps you and your current employees to better understand how things are being done in your company and to become more efficient. Having these Systems in place also makes for an easier and more efficient process when you bring new people into your organization. You have 'machinery' that works, effectively and efficiently.

What you care about now is **becoming a Superstar Company**. By 'Superstar', I mean being the best in your niche. If you think of your industry as a pyramid, there is only one company on top, a few on the second layer, then the third, and so on… until the bottom, where you find plenty of companies. Your Objective is to **get as close as possible to the top**. Why? Because if anything destructive happens in the economy or in your industry, or if anything happens that can adversely affect your business, you hardly feel it if you are on top. The financial crisis in 2008 resulted in many companies going bankrupt or being close to bankrupt – this is because they were at the bottom of the pyramid in their niche. If a tsunami comes, or the state does construction on the road in front of your shop or office, you need to be in such a strong position that your business does not suffer. This is being a Superstar Company.

After Systems are in place, you need to focus on **Innovation** if you want to take your company to the next level, in which case you go back to Sales in another growth cycle. Alternatively, you retire or sell your company (or you leave it as is and continue to manage 'in the business', which may eventually go downhill).

> *Shift Focus as your company develops and grows*

TAKE ACTION NOW!

Based on the Stage of your business development, decide which of the three areas discussed above requires your Focus. Write it down:

_____
_____
_____
_____
_____
_____

What are your biggest current Challenges? Write these here; then use the tactics in this book to find ways of overcoming these Challenges.

Challenge 1:
_____
_____

Challenge 2:
_____
_____

Challenge 3:
_____
_____

Challenge 4:
_____
_____

Challenge 5:
_____
_____

Take that Giant Leap

Tactic #87 — Take that Giant Leap

Embrace Innovation

Innovation is about doing something new or in a new way. You see Innovation all around you. Let's compare the lives of our great-grandparents with our lives today. How many new things do we have, and how many things are being done differently? If we want to visit a friend, we drive. If the friend lives far away, we catch a flight. If we have a question, we ask Google. If we want to buy a painting from Bali, we transfer the money online and the painting is shipped directly to our house. These are just examples of basic conveniences we have these days.

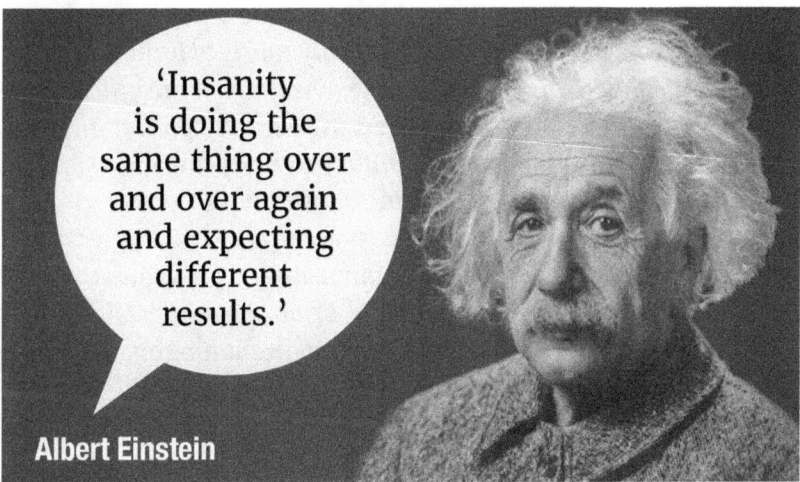

'Insanity is doing the same thing over and over again and expecting different results.'
Albert Einstein

But what are all these conveniences other than New Solutions to old problems? The Need to see a friend, the Need to get answers, the Need to decorate your house... Now think about the Solutions YOU provide. Think about the problems you solve for your customers. Is there any other way to solve the same problem? When you come up with another Solution, you are innovating. You either invent a new product, or you deliver an existing product in a different way. This is Innovation.

When I say embrace Innovation, I don't mean you necessarily have to invent something completely new. (Of course, if you can, that would be great.) The minimum you can do (and should do) is to use Innovation within your existing business. Be aware of New Solutions, and implement them quickly. Various adjustments to what you do may also lead to that big leap into greater success.

Make it work for you!

> *You run a restaurant. You think: 'People will always eat out, so I don't care about Innovation. I just need an oven, plates and cutlery.' I challenge you to consider that people's tastes change – so you need to revisit your menu. Thanks to Technology, the way restaurants communicate with their customers and market is changing too, so you need to consider new ways of reaching your customers. I have seen restaurants where guests place the order electronically and the waiter's only role is to bring the food to the table. This is 'cool' for the guests and more efficient for the restaurant. Many restaurants use various applications and devices to take the order, monitor inventory and even store information about recipes. Such restaurants haven't created anything new per se, but they are using the latest discoveries to increase their efficiency. They are innovating. This allows them to give more Value to the customer or brings greater profits to the owner, both of which are equally important for Long-Term Success.*

Do you want to take that leap? Do you want to massively grow your business? Because either you get lucky or you innovate. **If you want better results, you need to do something better – or differently.** If you want massive increase, you need to make high-impact changes (and remember: sometimes a small change can have greater impact than a big one).

Think about it: if you take the same road to get to work every day, you see pretty much the same things every day. Change your route and you will have a different perspective. You may see a new restaurant and decide to take your family there for Sunday brunch, or you may see a cool shop, or a house that inspires you to make an improvement to your own house.

If you want massive increase, make high-impact changes.

In your business, use Innovation to achieve better results. In order to innovate, you need to be open to exploring New Ideas, be ready to collaborate and develop the ability to commercialize New Ideas quickly. **Embed a 'yes' attitude and mindset. Seize the opportunity to try new things without fear of failure.** Every interaction you have with your team and with your customers is an experiment. Every idea is an opportunity to collaborate on creating something unique.

It took Innovation and being open to New Ideas to get my business to where it is today – a quite different and more successful organization to the one I started. When I realized I was in the wrong industry and needed to add other services to my company, I put together a collection of Business Best Practices used by the most successful companies in the world, and used these on our clients, to help them grow even Smarter Businesses. However, I wanted to be able to expand my company without being dependent on the quality or moods of the consultants I employed. This is how I came up with the idea of building an automatic tool using those Best Practices and identifying the growth potential for our clients and their companies.

Once I had it clear in my mind that the tool would work automatically, I asked myself how I could use this tool to greater impact, to help more small businesses grow. This is how **Business Lens™** became available online; it is for any business owner who wants to grow his company. So, based on my Need (or desire) to grow my consulting practice, I ended up creating a tool to be used online by lots of other business owners to grow their companies. This concept revolutionizes the entire consulting industry; it replaces a lot of manpower with Technology. I am now moving from consulting towards an internet startup: Tooliers.com will be the place where any small business owner will come to get on the right path to growing their company, building a Smarter Business and reaching their objectives faster. This is a huge jump!

TAKE ACTION NOW!

Write down 5 ways you could innovate in your business. These could be 5 actions you haven't considered before, or 5 avenues to explore… anything you can think of!

1. _____
_____
_____

2. _____
_____
_____

3. _____
_____
_____

4. _____
_____
_____

5. _____
_____
_____

Tactic #88

Learn from Startups

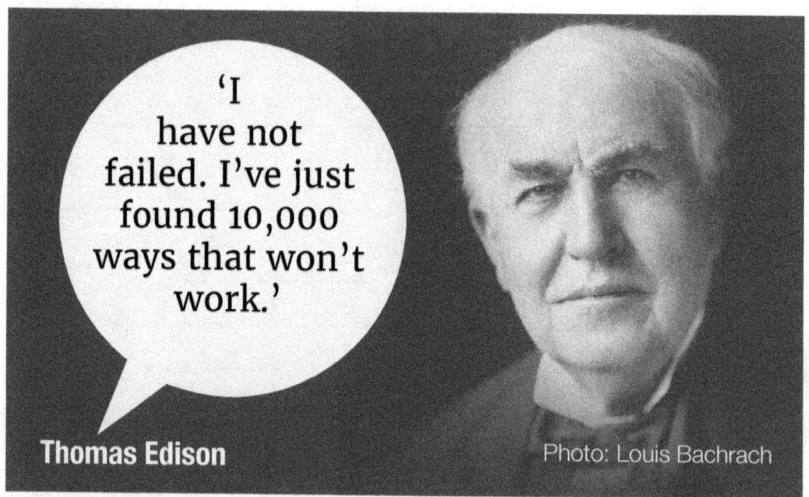

'I have not failed. I've just found 10,000 ways that won't work.'

Thomas Edison Photo: Louis Bachrach

Got an idea? Go for it. No, I'm not saying invest loads of money building something no one may want. Experiment first. Pivot. Do little things and test them with your customers. Since you are a business, you have customers. So each time you have an idea simply ask your customers what they think about it. If you don't have enough customers, or your customers are the wrong type for the New Idea, talk to your business partners or suppliers. If needs be, talk to your neighbors, your team, and even your team's family if they are relevant to your new product!

'During my 3 years with no sales but only struggle to make ANY sale on Tooliers, I discovered 1,000 ways that lead to dead ends in 21st century.'

If they like it, develop it into a concept product; i.e. a product on paper. Only try to sell it to your targeted customers. Only build the product after you have paying customers.

Startups operate on a shoestring budget, yet many are successful in building multi-million dollar Sales. What characteristics do they all have? A Passion for what they do, a motivated team and (very) limited Resources. Can you replicate this? Set up an experiment. Put a team together and give them a project (of course, the team members have to be relevant to the project). Get them to run the project independently from anything else going on in your company. Give them a limited budget, a limited set of Resources and an audacious Goal to achieve within a certain timeframe. Be prepared to accept failure! Not all startups succeed.

Have regular meetings with your project team and be the objective critical eye. If they don't convince you, it may not be the right project. Then reconsider it, or ditch it. Go with your gut feeling, if this is what you relied on when you started your current business. Be prepared to change direction if necessary. Most startups end up in a totally different place than what they expected. Flexibility is key.

If you don't want to be so ambitious as to conquer the world with your New Idea, you can make incremental changes to what you are already doing. Treat every change as an experiment. If the results are positive, the experiment is a success and you move to the next step. If the results are not positive, you either go back one step, or you change direction completely.

**Experiment, learn, improve.
Try again, closer to desired outcome.
Learn. Tweak. Succeed.**

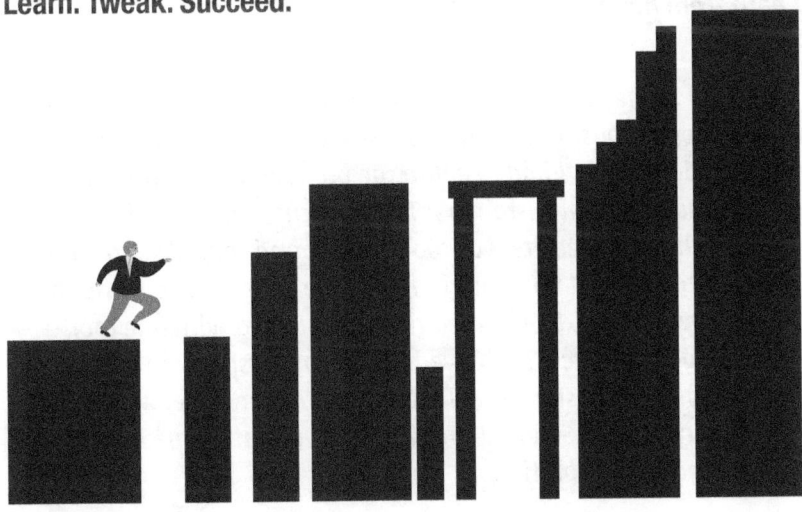

'From plan A to the plan that works.'

Ash Maurya — Photo: Angélica Martínez

I like the lean startup philosophy quoted above. Innovation is about the new, the unknown, uncertainty. Don't expect things to be predictable and happen as they do in your traditional business. Make changes, adjust until you make it work – as long as you have the market confirmation: that there is a demand for what you are trying to do, and that people are prepared to pay for the Solution you are developing.

Step-by-step changes and experiments will help you get the right product to market, and in the right way.

Learn from my mistake

> *I wasted money on building a platform with 16 tools for various aspects of the business – only to discover afterwards that no one used any of it. I had to get to the point of failure to start talking to potential customers. These discussions helped me realize that the website was too complex and complicated, and that customers did not want to invest the time to read through and understand it. So I binned that and started with one tool, which I gave for free. I achieved a 14% conversion rate (a great number) in the first weeks of launching the new site, which was extremely simple. So I had the market's validation: people were interested in my Solution.*

However, although my Solution was a diagnostic tool that would tell business owners where they needed to focus to grow their businesses, it didn't tell them how to achieve this. Based on Customer Feedback (yep, this time I was smarter and talked to them), I understood that they wanted something more. They wanted the how to grow their business and fix the problems. So I developed the concept of Fast Track Implementation Plan. I put it on the site, and my conversion rate decreased to 1%. This is because the site was too confusing (again). Fortunately I had installed a monitoring tool and could see the user's behavior on the site. Based on their clicks, I understood what they were interested in, and what was unclear. I made some improvements and my conversion went up to 5% – not as good as the first one, but better than 1%. As I was still not getting the results I wanted, I spoke to the potential customers again. Those conversations helped me redesign my offering, until I managed to get it right and get driven entrepreneurs and small business owners to buy.

TAKE ACTION NOW!

Think of an area that's not performing as well as you hoped it would. Write down 5 experiments you will undertake to attempt to improve it:

1. _____
   _____
   _____

2. _____
   _____
   _____

3. _____
   _____
   _____

4. _____
   _____
   _____

5. _____
   _____
   _____

Create a Startup Environment

> *Be cool, relaxed and fun.*
> *If you are too stiff yourself,*
> *allow your team to be cool, relaxed and fun*

Startups are amazing at achieving great results with small teams and limited Resources. The main ingredient for their success is the Culture and environment that the founders create. Why would you not replicate that in your organization? If not for the entire company, then at least for the team that works on the Innovation project? This is exactly what Steve Jobs did. Apple's epic success, the Macintosh, started as a small side project that had insignificant Resources compared to Apple's mainstream project at the time, the Lisa computer.

Ten ways to imitate a startup

1. **Promote a creative environment.** Encourage your employees to be innovative and implement their personal ideas. By creative environment I mean 'openness', but also the right working space. You may create a separate office for the Innovation team, or you may like to send them for an offsite meeting somewhere unusual to stimulate their creativity and remove them from their daily routine.

2. **Make work schedules flexible.** Startups don't have fixed schedules. You cannot say to your team: now is the time to be creative. Some people are more creative during the night, others get their best ideas while running in the park. Give your Innovation team the freedom to create. No schedule! Of course, you want to know they are doing the work, so you do need some structure and Accountability.

3. **Have transparent communication.** Encourage your staff to share their ideas, bad or good. This sharing has to come from the top. You need to be the first to share. Improve communication within your company by creating transparency and ensuring your employees feel comfortable speaking with top management.

4. **Praise your employees for their accomplishments.** Startups don't have money to pay bonuses, but they nonetheless have very committed people. One reason is that the achievements of the team or individual are recognized. Tell employees that they are doing a great job, that you appreciate their work. This Motivation can buy you a lot more commitment than a bonus would.

5. **Allow room for growth.** Gone are the times when people were promoted based on the number of years they had worked in a position. If someone is good, promote them! They deserve it! Plus, they will maintain their Motivation and will be even more dedicated to your company.

6. **Challenge your employees.** Startups provide challenges every day for the team, which then constantly learns and develops. Why not trust your staff and provide them with more challenges? Help them grow and they will contribute even more. Keep them on the edge with new challenges.

7. **Encourage continuous learning.** Startups learn constantly – often from their mistakes and failures. You don't need your team to fail to learn, though. They can attend courses, or work in various departments to expand their mind, skills and understanding.

8. **Create an appealing work environment.** Startup teams love to work. Be it in their garage, their kitchen or in a park. Create a fantastic environment for your staff. Bring a pool table into the main office, or offer them a massage every Friday. Step out of the comfort zone of the established company and behave differently.

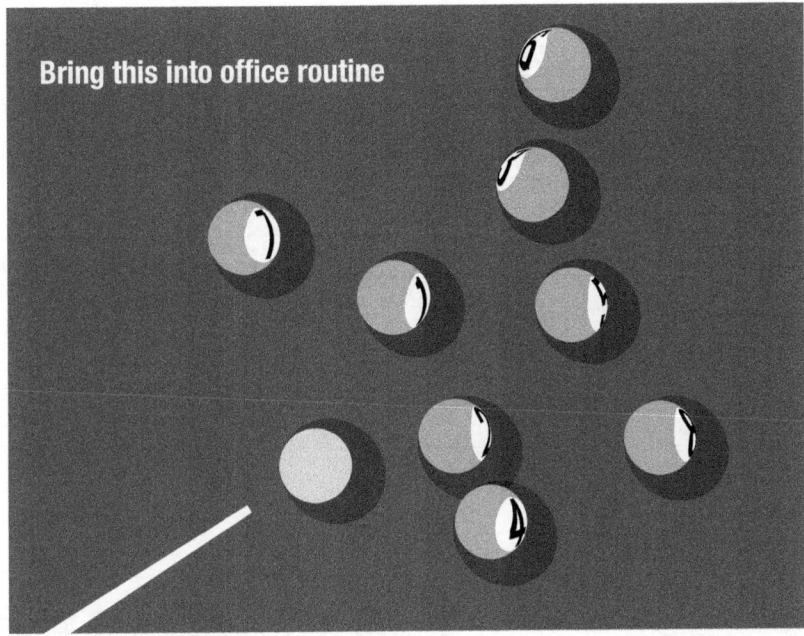

Bring this into office routine

9. **Work hard, play hard.** Take your team out, have fun. Celebrate achievements. Encourage them to let their hair down and party. Stiffness is for the boardroom, not for everyday life.

10. **Ask for input.** Startups value this from their employees. Whether you're making a change to the company or looking for advice on how to improve Sales, ask your employees for ideas. Ask them to provide Feedback during your decision-making process.

TAKE ACTION NOW!

Write down 5 actions you will take in the next 30 days to create a more relaxed and creative working environment at your company.

1. _____
_____
_____

2. _____
_____
_____

3. _____
_____
_____

4. _____
_____
_____

5. _____
_____
_____

Tactic #90

Follow Your Passion

Explore further what you like doing, and create products around that

What are you passionate about? Why did you initially start your business? What is your biggest Passion?

Recently I had a conversation with a man whose business was dying. In fact, it was not even a proper business: just a website that was generating a little money, enough for the owner to hang on and hope. He had realized though that he needed to do something else. He kept telling me he didn't know what that might be; that he had tried everything possible. During that conversation, I asked him for Feedback on my website. He was brilliant. He was able to tell me things that no highly paid consultants had spotted. I made a comment about his abilities to

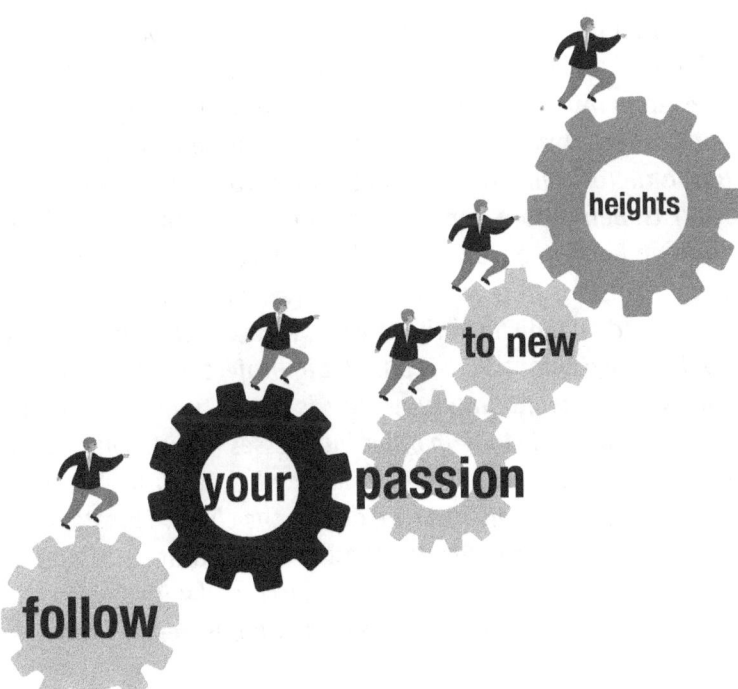

criticize websites and he admitted that this is what he loves doing. This is his Passion. Would you not want someone like him to critique your website, so that you could know exactly what to improve and how to provide a better experience for your customer?

He went on to set up a new business doing exactly this: assessing websites. He is now combining his Passion with a big Need in the market, and he is making much more money than what he was making with his previous website. All it took was one conversation!

If you are not passionate about your product, if you just started your business because you saw an opportunity, and today you are making money, that's fine. But you must be passionate about something you do in that business. It could be that you like talking to your customers, or that you like choosing your raw materials... whatever it is, identify it, and think how you can do more and better with what you enjoy doing.

Let me tell you my story...

In 2004 I set up a consulting firm as a 'bridge' between the UK and Romania. There were a lot of business people in the UK interested in my help and Romanian connections. They were looking for anything from setting up a new production facility in Romania to buying an existing business to employing IT specialists. Being from Romania and having had my professional training in London gave me the edge to develop a successful business. This business was based on my connections, skills and abilities, and on a niche in the market, where there was clearly a Need. But the economic crisis put all big projects on hold and my business almost went bankrupt... this is when I realized that my Passion was actually to help other businesses make money; that I was most thrilled when a project succeeded, because that is when I saw the Value in what we did for the client. This Passion, combined with a large library of Best Practices that successful businesses apply led to me being very successful with Tooliers®, my online platform with tools to help small businesses grow.

Although I didn't start out with any Passion as such (see above), I discovered my Passion later and aligned my business with it. It is only then that I achieved success. Before that, I made a decent living, but I couldn't really call it a successful business. The Breakthrough came when I could put my finger on my Passion and use it to serve others.

> *Small tweaks in your business can bring your passion back!*

If you are not sure how to build a business around your passion, access our online Master Class, "Design Your Business Model Based on Your Needs & Passions" *(www.ozanagiusca.com/your-business-model/)*.

This Master Class empowers you to identify your Power Spot – which is determined by your passion, your skills and abilities and based on what people desperately want. By the end of this Master Class, and in just five steps, you will have identified exactly what to sell, based on what YOU need and where the money is.

I see an increasing number of clients using our tools and participating in our programs who have well established businesses which generate enough money for them to do what they want, when they want. And they develop other businesses based on their Passions, which give them the kick, the edge. Those businesses require much more focus, energy, thinking than the original business. But they do it with so much more pleasure than working in their existing (traditional) business!

There is another type of clients, those entrepreneurs who want to grow their sales and profits, and when they work with us they discover other ways of generating money, related to their existing business, and most importantly based on their Passion.

Bottom line: you can have both the money and the Passion. And you SHOULD have both!

Your objective...

TAKE ACTION NOW!

Identify your Passion(s):

_____
_____
_____

Write down 5 ideas to connect your Passion to your business, or to connect your business to your Passion:

1. _____
_____
_____

2. _____
_____
_____

3. _____
_____
_____

4. _____
_____
_____

5. _____
_____
_____

Tactic #91

Take that Giant Leap

Bring New Voices into Your Company

By New Voices I mean new people from outside of the company who generate different thinking, different perspectives, and different views. Anyone can be a New Voice. Really! It could be the teller when you do your weekly groceries shopping, or a highly regarded businessperson. You may be surprised to find that your child can generate a New Perspective for you, or can trigger an idea for a new product. Of course, the quality of the New Voice influences the quality of the information you receive.

> *Even people you think are less qualified to give you advice can help. You never know where the great idea will come from. Be open!*

The best New Voices are usually consultants, coaches or trainers. But you can also just have a monthly meeting with a few of your friends

who run other types of businesses and exchange ideas. Make a habit of sharing what works in each business, and try to apply those techniques in your business. Alternatively, use Tooliers.com, which shows you the whole picture of your company and what you lack for further growth. It also gives you step-by-step actions to implement the latest business concepts and discoveries into your business, based on your specific Needs (which are uncovered during the diagnosis).

An example of bringing together New Voices is my Ozana's Inner Circle™ *(www.ozanagiusca.com/inner-circle)*, which gives members a new perspective on their business via various events they join, and in addition they are part of a community on Facebook (closed group available only to my clients), where they can ask any question. Myself and members of the community answer those questions. This is one way... but there is another way to bring New Voices in the business. And that is by participating in our Expert Lounges - these are online meetings available to the members of the Inner Circle, where each member asks questions and gets live answers from me and from the other participants. The beauty of these sessions is that participants get more for their business from listening to others' questions. Because they hear new questions that they hadn't thought about, new ideas that they could also implement in their businesses.

Don't try to do everything by yourself; it is simply impossible. New Voices can bring New Perspectives, make you see things you had not considered before. **You may get an idea that can bring thousands or millions of dollars in additional Sales for your business.** Or you may get an idea that can save thousands or millions for your business. Or you may simply save a lot of time for yourself.

Don't overlook a potential New Voice

A student told me in early 2000 that I had to blog. My reaction was: "Who are you? Why would I waste time writing, when I could use my time on something else?" What I am doing now? Blogging! Would I have been further ahead of Competitors if I had listened to him at the time? Yes!

Since I've come to understand how important it is to bring New Voices into my business, I am always open to observing, to talking to people. I know a lot about business, and I constantly add to my Knowledge.

Now we're talking!

> I'd mastered Facebook and LinkedIn for Marketing and Sales, but I still didn't get Twitter. Recently I met with an entrepreneur in Belgium who had seen one of my presentations. We had an exploratory discussion, and we both learned from each other: I shared some tricks we use on Facebook (he loved them!) and he shared tips on using Twitter. If, at the time of reading this book, I have a significant number of followers, it worked! (Follow me @OzanaGiusca)

TAKE ACTION NOW!

Write down 5 New Voices you will bring into your business (e.g. seeing a consultant or advisor, participating in a Training workshop, chatting to a partner about each other's business Challenges, or checking out Tooliers®.)

1. _____
_____
_____

2. _____
_____
_____

3. _____
_____
_____

4. _____
_____
_____

5. _____
_____
_____

Tactic #92

Take that Giant Leap

Bring in Experts

You know your company inside out. You may even know your industry inside out. But you can't know everything about business in general. These days, everything is changing so fast, that is impossible for one person to keep up with everything. Skills are highly specialized these days. If you want to master everything, you can't apply anything. You will spend so much time on learning that you won't have time to implement.

> *You can try to become an Expert in everything, but is it worth the time you spend learning about the subject?*

You have an accountant, right? Do you follow how tax rules and other legislation change, or do you rely on your accountant to tell you and to implement them in your business? Surely the latter (unless this is a real interest of yours)! Why not rely on other Experts in very specialized fields to broaden your horizon and help you take your business to the next level?

Here's why you need to do this!

> Consider the case of a famous architect who needs a new website. He doesn't know how to build websites and his team members don't know either. His best Solution is to outsource this task to an Expert. The Expert may charge the architect more than what he earns (if he considers the hourly rate), but could he do this work himself? If he were to learn website development, he would spend a lot more time on the project, and it would end up even more expensive. He needs to accept paying for (what appears to be expensive) outside help to get the job done, while he focuses on what he is good at: designing houses.

Take that Giant Leap

The only area you can't rely on experts alone is marketing and sales

If you want great results from experts you need to master it so you know what to ask from them

From my professional experience, I find that the strengths of a company tend to align with the owner's Skills and Passions. If the owner is good at creating products, the company will have a great product. But the same owner can't necessarily sell – so the company may find it barely sells its great products. The owner who is great at selling may be a disaster when it comes to organizing – and so his company will be weak in this area. No individual knows it all or can do it all, or is good at it all. Companies are the same. There are only a few companies in the world that are good at everything – and you know them: brands like Google, Apple, Amazon, Coca-Cola.

If you want to be good at everything and become big and famous, you need to first understand what you are not good at and address those areas (remember Tactic #37 'Strengthen the Weakest Link'?). Either develop Expertise in-house, or bring it in from outside. Give the jobs you are bad at to people who are top of that class, and your business will thrive. I don't agree that we have to work on improving everything we are bad at. **For maximum efficiency and best results, bring in people who are passionate about those areas, and let *them* improve your business.**

I once met a self-made millionaire who subcontracted almost everything. When I asked if he had studied law to draft such great contracts, he said he employed great lawyers. When I asked if he read his own financial results, he said he had a great CFO that did it for him. When I asked him if he skis, he said: 'No, I have others do it for me, so I can enjoy this glass of wine with you.'

Do it right!

> *What do you know about video marketing? At the time of writing this book, YouTube is the SEO Wild Wild West. With the right technique, anyone on YouTube can bring loads of traffic to their website. Do you know that you can also have (almost) free advertising on YouTube? If you put a video up there advertising your service and choose to pay per click, you only pay if someone watches your video for more than 30 seconds. If the person clicks 'skip ad' before 30 seconds – and most people do – you don't pay anything. If someone watches more than 30 seconds, you pay. But you have a qualified Lead and that is something worth paying for.*

So now you know what you need to do: shoot a video, upload it to YouTube, create a campaign for it, and watch the traffic coming to your website. Sounds simple right? But it's only simple if you're an Expert and know how to do it. Try do it yourself: by the time you have figured it all out, YouTube may have changed the rules. You either move fast and do it properly – through an Expert – or you miss an opportunity.

> *Use the best Expert in the field. Pay more than you had expected. It is worth the investment*

BUT...

Whenever you use experts, I would highly suggest you make an effort to understand the strategic elements.

What do I mean?

Well, you don't need to know how to make a video or how to get traffic from YouTube. But it is your full responsibility to think strategically about your business. It is your responsibility to decide the objective of that video and how that video will be used for maximum impact and best results. It is your responsibility to work with your team to design the Customer's Journey so that when you get Leads from YouTube, they convert into paying clients. You cannot rely on the YouTube specialist to make the sale for you!

What I'm saying is that you need to be on top of all the specialists you employ, you need to coordinate them. Ok, you may have someone in your team coordinate them, but only after you have understood the basics and you have agreed the strategy with your colleague in charge.

I wish I knew this when I was paying big money to experts expecting them to come with the miracle to reach the sales I wanted. It cost me almost half a million in training programs, courses, masterminds, hiring people and experts, building our platform, paying for advertising and other such activities, to realize that no one wants my business to reach the sky other than me. And I can't blame them for this! Every expert is just focused on their task. Most experts don't think of my strategy, they don't even care or they don't understand it. This is why it is so important that you, the owner of the business, design your strategy, understand every tactic you need, and THEN get experts to do things for you.

If you are not on top of these things, experts will simply not deliver the results you want! And it is not their fault...

> *Develop your strategy THEN give it to experts to implement!*

TAKE ACTION NOW!

Write down 5 areas in your business which could do with external Expertise:

1. _____
   _____
   _____

2. _____
   _____
   _____

3. _____
   _____
   _____

4. _____
   _____
   _____

5. _____
   _____
   _____

Tactic #93 — Take that Giant Leap

Bring the Person(s) You Need into Your Business Today

> *Bring in an outside person*
> *who is hungry and has high ambitions*

You may have built a successful company and reached a plateau. Your business may be growing but not at the double or triple digits you want. You have got New Voices that generated New Ideas and now it is time to implement these. Your options are to use existing Resources or to recruit new people. Which do you go for?

Bring the person(s) you need into your business today

I encourage you to be brave and recruit. You want a big jump, right? Those already in your company are used to a certain way of doing things. They are comfortable where they are and it is not easy to change people. Besides, you recruited them for the existing jobs, or even for old jobs that changed over time. Right now, you need fresh blood in your business.

Bring someone from outside who has the drive you have. Of course you want the Skills, but you also want the commitment and the hard work. You want a can-do, unstoppable attitude. If everyone in your company has this attitude, then great, just promote some of your Resources to get involved with the new projects. But I doubt you have it. And if you do, you are ahead of me, and may not even need this book.

Take time to assess your company in the current economy, in your industry today. Your big plans may or may not be linked to your current activities. You may need New Skills. You may need some specialized expertise. You may need the latest discoveries in various business areas brought into your business. Unless your people have been continuously Trained and have kept up with new developments in fields that matter to your new projects, you are better off bringing in people from outside. **Consider bringing in a combination of employees and short-term Experts.** The Experts may cost you more per hour or job, but they do the right thing faster, and to high standards.

If you can bring in a new partner, this may be a good option. You may be tempted to keep the whole pie for yourself, but it is best to have a smaller part of a bigger pie than to have 100% of a small pie. You want to share responsibilities as well as the glory. You want a partner who may be keener even than you are! Someone fresh! That person brings the execution, the implementation, but also more ideas and viewpoints.

Recruit or die...

I was in a situation where I either recruited or my business would go downhill. Why? Because my small team was being maxed out emotionally. Let me explain. When I switched from our traditional consulting business to a new way of supporting small businesses and delivering our knowledge in a way that people were not yet used to, I lost some of my employees. This is normal, as they wanted to continue doing the classic consulting projects. So I was left with four team members, each having developed a set of skills, all complementary. Six years later, one of my core team members left at a moment when we had too much work to do for us and for our clients. Her departure left many unresolved issues. This was also during the holiday period, when we were understaffed anyway. Additionally, we had been wanting to grow our team for over a year, by recruiting three juniors – the colleague who left was in charge of recruiting and she could not get some of the others to stay. I realised recently that it must have been a mission impossible for her to recruit someone long term, as she had been wanting to leave for over six months and her mind was no longer with us.

To cut a long story short, here we are, three people, really skilled and super smart, freaking out because no one knew the technicalities of the work that the person who left was doing. They were forced to quickly learn those technicalities, and they were not comfortable. The thought that they may be doing a bad job for clients placed a lot of stress on them. They wanted me to be fully available to help them with their daily tasks.

Did I do it?

No!

What did I do instead?

I sent an email to our subscribers list (yes, our subscribers are entrepreneurs but they have children, cousins and neighbours that they could introduce to work for us), generated 20 strong potential candidates, and hired four. Two joined us immediately, of which one was able to do the tech stuff that my former employee was doing (with a bit of training though), and my team instantly relaxed. The other two people are bringing in new ideas, they are helping us get more organised so that we deliver even better value to our clients, and now things look brighter than ever :)

TAKE ACTION NOW!

Write down 5 characteristics of the New Person you want to bring into your business today:

1. _____
_____
_____

2. _____
_____
_____

3. _____
_____
_____

4. _____
_____
_____

5. _____
_____
_____

Tactic #94

Fire the Person Holding You Back

A Good Employee yesterday may be a Bad Employee tomorrow

People have always been, and probably will always be, one of the most important assets to any organization. At the same time, people can be the biggest problem in an organization.

Keeping an employee who isn't contributing positively can really hurt your company, especially if you have a small business in which Culture is closely tied to success. **A Bad Employee can be a rotten apple in your company.** Strong negativity, poor attitude, backbiting and incompetence can spread quickly within your company. Co-workers typically try to fight off or resist catching the negative traits, but these tend to be contagious and can severely hurt or even kill a company. Besides, the employee is holding the place of someone else who could truly contribute and help the team.

Any one of your employees can become a Bad Employee for multiple reasons: they may be resistant to change, they may not like the new direction, or they may need change, which your company is not providing. They could simply get bored in their job, or acquire other interests or require more challenges... Analyze your employees constantly and change them if they are no longer appropriate for your business. Of course, try to identify the cause of the mismatch first and try to fix it. If this is not possible, break the bond and offer yourself, your team and that person an exit from a poor working environment.

Here's why you need to do this!

I once had a great consultant who managed to find creative Solutions for most of our projects. He brought business in, managed project delivery, and really helped everyone in the

company. He had been with us for seven years and he knew everything about our business. He was extremely valuable. However, when I came in with New Ideas, although he liked them, he wasn't keen to be involved. Within months he became resistant. He simply shut himself off from the new direction I wanted the company to take and started finding faults in everything we were doing.

My advisers told me to fire him. But I couldn't. They told me that his lack of Motivation and bad attitude would rub off on other employees. I understood this, and I saw it happening, but I still could not let him go. He had been with us for so long – a lot of our achievements were due to his contribution. How could I let go of such a great person? What about our personal connection? Our relationship had gone beyond employee–employer. We went skiing together, we attended parties and other social activities, we even made some investments together.

Bad employee

One year later and I still had no results from this employee. I had to do something – so I gave him targets to accomplish within the new direction, which meant he had to accept the new direction and deliver, or he wouldn't get paid. Unfortunately, he didn't deliver, and thus he didn't get paid. Within a month, he had left. Today he does what he was doing for us in another company. He is happy doing what he wants to do – and we are happy about not having to carry someone who doesn't contribute.

Some experts may say that when someone is no longer performing you should identify what has happened and help that person go over the challenges so the motivation returns and performance goes back up. In reality I believe it rarely happens. Once someone has switched off, it is difficult to get them excited about your business again, so going our separate ways is the best solution. If you are like me and you treat your employees as your family, it may be hard to accept, but it is best for all parties involved. Of course, it is even better that you ensure your employees are motivated and committed all the time (See Tactic #45 Maximize Your Team's Commitment)

I realize that whenever I lost great employees, those losses led me to find others even better. So don't be afraid to replace your employees if they are no longer 100% with you.

> *Fire immediately when you realize an employee is no longer a good fit*

TAKE ACTION NOW!

Identify 3 people within your company who you consider to be Bad Employees or a bad influence. Mention why for each person.

1. _____
   _____
   _____

2. _____
   _____
   _____

3. _____
   _____
   _____

4. _____
   _____
   _____

5. _____
   _____
   _____

Tactic #95

Take that Giant Leap

Know TODAY. Anticipate TOMORROW

Just as you wouldn't sell horses for transportation, as the car has been invented and does a better job, you wouldn't want to set up a large national newspaper today, because the trend is towards digital media. You may have the best product on the planet, but if the world has moved away from using that type of product, your business will die.

> *Know exactly where your industry is today*

As a business owner, you must understand what is going on not just in your own business but also in your entire industry. Reflect regularly on your industry to understand what Stage it is at right now, and where it is heading. Understand the industry challenges of both today and tomorrow.

Make it work for you!

> Travel agencies have suffered since the advent of the internet. People are now booking flights, accommodation and even complete holidays online. There is no need to speak to a travel agent anymore. The information is available online. Unless you are in a niche market, or offer high-end holidays, it is highly likely you will be out of business soon. But what if you anticipated this change five years ago, or even 10 years ago? Maybe you would be Booking.com!

Don't hide from the truth: the factors that affect the entire industry do (or will) have an impact on your business. While you arguably can't control these external factors, you can control how your business will respond to them. Such factors can hurt you – or they can help you, if you know how to use them to your advantage.

Anticipate TOMORROW

Do you like your industry? Can your business produce the results you expect in your industry? These are other questions you need to ask yourself. You may remember that my consulting company used to help organizations in Romania get EU funding (grants for investment projects to help the country develop faster). Despite the potential for huge consulting fees, I realized this is not a good industry to be in. Why? Not because of Competition or New Technologies, but because the system is dysfunctional and the Romanian authorities incompetent. This is unlikely to change. The result is that nothing is predictable, that a professional service becomes a lottery. You may do a great job, and still not get grants for your clients because the people working in the system do not follow clear rules and procedures.

As mentioned earlier, another drawback of this industry is that you alternate between times of high-intensity work and times of almost no work. So you have peaks in which your Resources (staff) are stretched, and then you have lows, when your consultants have nothing to do.

It was clear to me that a consulting business cannot be sustainable in this industry. This is when I came up with the **Business Doctor** service: we perform a diagnosis on companies to identify where they are leaving money on the table, make a plan with them to grow their business, and help them implement it. With this **Complementary Service**, we have constant work for our consultants. In EU funding peak times the entire team is busy with preparing projects for grant proposals and in between calls for proposals, our consultants work on **Business Doctor.**

> Know exactly where your company is
> in its industry today

If I had failed to really see the dynamics of the EU grant proposal industry in Romania, and not come up with a future-oriented Solution, the business today would be a struggle to survive – we would be covering the low months (losses) with the profits from peak months.

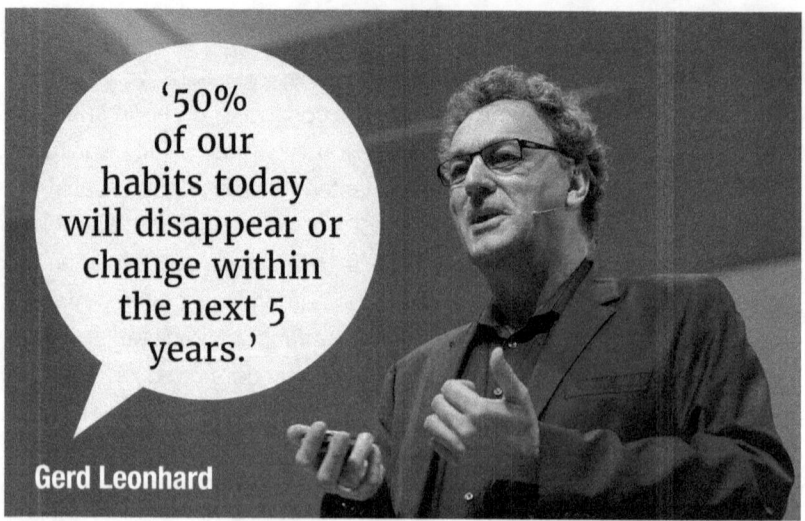

'50% of our habits today will disappear or change within the next 5 years.'

Gerd Leonhard

Once you understand the nuts and bolts of your industry, reflect on where your company is within that industry. In most industries there are no heroes, just choices. So rather than trying to be all things to all people, position your company in your niche, and aim to dominate that niche.

Now we're talking! They're already doing it!

Our tools on Tooliers® perform miracles on businesses that want to grow, businesses that are suffering or businesses that don't know where they are. The same tools can be used by the small business owner and by managers in larger companies. The tools can even be used by banks, private equity funds, rating agencies and many other organizations. When we launched Tooliers®, we were the Solution for everything and everyone. And we sold nothing! Once we took one niche – small business owners committed to growing their companies and who have minimum time and capital to invest in growth – we were able to craft targeted messages, which attracted attention. This is how we managed to raise interest in the market and then to sell.

Take that Giant Leap

I challenge you to think What happens to your business if...

1. The habit generating the need for your product or service disappears?

2. The habit generating the need for your clients' product or service disappears?

3. The way people buy changes and your marketing and sales activities are no longer generating any customer?

TAKE ACTION NOW!

Write down 5 characteristics of your industry TODAY:

1. _____
_____
_____

2. _____
_____
_____

3. _____
_____
_____

4. _____
_____
_____

5. _____
_____
_____

Write down 5 characteristics you think your industry will have in the FUTURE:

1. _____

_____

_____

2. _____

_____

_____

3. _____

_____

_____

4. _____

_____

_____

5. _____

_____

_____

Identify Your Prospects' Needs Even Before They Do

> Constantly observe your customers' behavior
>
> Look at what makes them happy and what makes them anxious

If you want to take that big leap forward, you have to **anticipate what your customers will want in future**. This is one of the secrets to the success of Steve Jobs. If he had gone out and asked people whether they wanted an iPad, the answer would have been 'no'. Clients were not aware of their Need. It is Steve Jobs who anticipated and perhaps even created this Need!

A smart application!

> Think back to 10 years ago. You had a phone and a camera. And a computer. The phone's job was to make phone calls; to enable you to speak to people not in your vicinity. The camera's job was to take pictures, so you could have memories of places you had visited and people you had met. The computer's job was a little more complex: you could work on Word documents, you could perform calculus and create graphs in Excel, you could create presentations in PowerPoint, you could access the internet, access emails and more. Today, you have smart phones that perform all these jobs.

Did you imagine 10 years ago that one day your whole 'life' would be in one device? Can you imagine your life now without a smart phone? Your Need changed and those companies that anticipated this change are doing very well.

In 2015 I participated in an exercise at a high profile event, in which I had to use customer interviews to identify the characteristics of the future fridge. A fridge is a fridge, right? You store food inside, to preserve it for longer. But when I performed the customer interviews, I was amazed to discover that the majority of interviewees wanted their fridge to do the following: tell me when supplies have run out, tell me when items are about to expire, prepare the meal for me, serve the meal for me.

What's interesting is that none of the people I interviewed had thought of these functions before. Only when I challenged them to tell me what job(s) they would like the fridge to perform, did they reach these conclusions. I dare say there is clearly a Need or a gap in the market for such a fridge! Their reasons were varied: from saving time to relieving the stress of preparing a meal for the family. The fridge manufacturer now knows to design tomorrow's fridge – and he also knows the key elements of his marketing messages.

> *What does your 'tomorrow product' look like? The answer to this question comes once you have identified your clients' Future Needs.*

Do you recognize any of these companies? They are all new and very successful. Why? Because they solve old problems in a new way.

Think about your business: How can you solve a particular problem your clients face, in a different way?

TAKE ACTION NOW!

Write down 5 problems your customers are facing right now (these don't have to be those problems for which you are currently providing Solutions, think of problems relevant to your industry).

1. _____
_____
_____

2. _____
_____
_____

3. _____
_____
_____

4. _____
_____
_____

5. _____
_____
_____

Tactic #97

Identify Your Clients' REAL Needs

> *Understand WHY people do what they do, not just what they say they do*

Up until a few years ago, if you'd asked a CD retailer why customers come to his shop, he would have said 'to buy the CD of their favorite singer'. Steve Jobs realized that they don't buy CDs – they buy music. He satisfied the same Need (to listen to music) in a different way: digital music. If he had sold pink CDs (provided that he wanted to satisfy the Need of buying CDs), would he have been as successful?

In most cases, people are not aware of their real Need...

When I initially developed Business Lens™, the tool to show the business owner the naked truth about his business, I asked my friends and existing clients to test it. When I asked a friend: 'What is your biggest business Challenge?' he replied that he didn't have any Challenges. He is well positioned, he has customers and he made money. He is doing okay. He just needs to spend most of his time in his pub, but this is the norm in the hospitality industry. If you are not there, the barman steals, the personnel do not clean properly, the waiters do not serve the guests well, and so on.

I asked him to do me a favor and go through the questions in my Business Lens™ and give me Feedback. He spent three hours with us and, when he saw the report, he could not believe it: he had many more problems than he had realized. And the real problem in his business was himself. All of the negative elements of his work were created by his way of thinking and his attitude towards his staff. He thought people in his industry would come and go, that they didn't deserve any Training, or special attention. On reading our report, he realized that it was possible to recruit the right people, and most importantly to develop the right Culture in his company, in order to accomplish his Goals. Now, he hardly spends time at the pub at all. He enjoys holidays, weekends away, time with his family, and his pub makes more money. In fact, he is in the process of opening a pub in another location.

The point is to identify the customers real Need, a Need that they are not aware of (mostly because they did not know any other way to do things). Do this by showing people their real problems. There is a difference between what clients want and what they truly need. Find out their underlying Needs, both present and future. This will help you remain relevant, and will lead to that big jump.

Assess your customer's Needs now.
Repeat once a year.

Why is Apple so successful?
Because they CREATE Needs

Members in my Inner Circle constantly come to me with questions like:
- How do I get more likes?
- How do I get more traffic?
- How do I get more clients?

These are good questions, but are not really what they need.

If you think about it, why do they want more likes? So they get more clients? Why do they want more traffic? So they get more clients? Why do they want more clients? So they increase their sales.

My point?

The real Need is increased sales. The problem? More likes don't lead to more sales. This is more like an ego boost - the business owner feels good because of the many likes.

How about traffic? You can get 30,000 clicks for $5. But is this helping your business? Definitely not. You need to answer the following questions:

1. How do I convert my traffic? Because when you figure out a way to convert traffic, you don't mind paying for it. More so, you want to constantly increase your promotion budget, because you know for sure you'll get your investment back, plus extra. The opposite is also true: when you don't convert your traffic, it is because you are not willing to pay for it. You expect free traffic, which is not really free and is very limited when you use SEO.

2. How do I get more and BETTER clients? Because let's face it: no business can serve everyone on this planet. So why not get more of the Best Clients, who are prepared to pay the right money, who are a pleasure to serve, and who are easy to acquire, simply to make your life easier? Because not many entrepreneurs think this way.

So?

This clearly demonstrates that people know what they want but don't really know what they need. Once I realized this, I was able to provide better service. Because every time I get a question from a client, I ask myself: What is behind this question? What does this person REALLY want?

And when I do this, I am able to really help them! Most often I start by rephrasing their questions to get them to realize they didn't ask the right question. And then we discuss the right answer to the right question.

But there is something hugely important in this! When you spot the wrong questions and figure out what the right questions are for your clients, you really understand what they are looking for, and what they need. Thus you can come up with a Solution that better satisfies your clients and generates more money for you. So it is a win-win for everyone.

> *Fill in the gap between your client's Wants and Needs*

TAKE ACTION NOW!

Write down 5 reasons your customers behave the way they do in relation to the type of product or service you offer:

1. _____
_____
_____

2. _____
_____
_____

3. _____
_____
_____

4. _____
_____
_____

5. _____
_____
_____

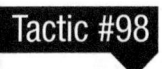

Take that Giant Leap

Leverage Your Platform for Maximum Results

By Platform I mean your infrastructure, and more. **Your Platform is everything that your company has today: people, assets, products / services, procedures, credentials, brand, reputation.** Think of what your business has, and how you can extract maximum Value from this.

I once met an investment fund manager at Cargill. I was curious to know how one could manage investment funds while working for an agricultural company. He explained that, because Cargill has **AAA rating**, they can borrow money very cheaply. So they set up an investment fund to make more money. The model is simple: based on their good borrowing capacity, they borrow money (which costs them very little) and use that money to invest in other assets, which make even more money for them; i.e. they Leverage their credibility and use their 'Platform' to make more money.

Ask yourself:

- What do we have?
- What else do our clients want?
- How can we serve our clients more?

And... How can we go beyond our customers or our traditional line of business?

You don't have to be a multinational company to apply this concept. You may be a small retailer of electronics. Your margins are small, because you can't afford to buy volumes from the supplier that command low prices. An idea for you is to buy a larger quantity, and sell the difference to another retailer just like you: you make a margin on that, as well as obtain a larger margin for your store. If this is not possible due to lack of funds, then associate with another retailer and make a Joint Purchase –

Business Unlimited

this doesn't require any additional investment on your side, but leads to lower prices due to the volume you buy together. Be creative!

How can you leverage the opportunities given by the Digital Transformation in the entire world?

This is what we like to see!

> At my company, our projects and applications for EU funding for clients became so good that people working in the ministry (whom we had never met) recommended us as consultants. We had no idea this was happening until we received a call from the largest car manufacturer in Romania requesting a meeting to discuss EU Funding. They had been referred to us by the ministry. This opened our eyes and we started actively encouraging authorities to spread the word about our company. This is an unconventional way to Leverage the good work we do, our credentials, the Platform we have, to bring more customers.

> *Leverage your Platform for now, but more so for the future*

TAKE ACTION NOW!

Write down 5 current qualities or strengths of your company that make up your Platform:

1. _____
2. _____
3. _____
4. _____
5. _____

Write down 5 ideas to further Leverage the above-mentioned strengths:

1. _____
_____
_____

2. _____
_____
_____

3. _____
_____
_____

4. _____
_____
_____

5. _____
_____
_____

Tactic #99

Expand Your Distribution Channels

Find creative ways to sell your product: Repackage and Repurpose your product for further reach

A Distribution Channel can refer to how you disseminate your product or service as well as new ways of selling your product. Repackaging or Repositioning your product, for example, might result in further reach.

This is how it's done!

As a car manufacturer, you would have to rely on one or more distributors in a territory. Let's imagine you have one distributor in New York, in Florida, and so on. Traditionally, you would get another distributor for the same territory, or you would go into a new country, where, again, you would look for local distributors. But how about using the internet as your distributor? Mini Cooper offer a great online application to design your own car. The interested buyer can select which features he wants the car to have, and can see the visual – and associated price – online. The distributor is not able to offer such a service, unless he uses the main website. With this tool on their website, BMW (who owns Mini Cooper) removes a fair amount of power from the distributor, as they generate leads online themselves.

...Or this

One of our clients imports and distributes consumable goods (plastic cups, tissues, garbage bags, to name but a few). They usually sell to large supermarkets, which constantly put pressure on price. So the client made a very clever move: they packaged some of their products for the hospitality industry and offered these online. They created their own Distribution Channel, for this specific target market. It's the same product, but they added Sales by addressing a new market, in a new way.

In case you haven't realized, I too am expanding my Distribution Channels – with this book. The library of Best Practices, which is the basis of **Business Lens™** (our main tool on Tooliers®) and some of the principles and concepts I share during my events are Repackaged here.

In fact, I treat this book as a teaser for so much more you can get from using our tools, participating in our Master Classes, bootcamps and various online programs. Consider this: traditionally, most businesses would reach their clients via third parties (e.g. a milk producer sells via supermarket, a software developer sells via a software integrator, a web designer sells via a marketing agency and the list continues). When you sell via a third party it is a great start, because for many businesses this would be the only way.

Now the new way is to talk directly to the customer, to have 'client ownership'. In other words, to have a direct communication channel with your customer, so you can hear what they have to say, so you can send your messages across, so you can send them your special offers and much more... which ultimately leads to more sales for you.

In the past, a juice producer would have no option. But today, you can have a direct relationship with your customer, thanks to the internet. And there is another way: via events. Yes, you can have a great reach when you organize events, because you can talk to many potential buyers at the same time, and most importantly, you can sell via events, which is an increasingly popular tool for Smart Business owners.

Consider leveraging the internet and events for your business, so you become in full control of your sales and ultimately of your profits.

When you develop your system to generate business via a combination of online marketing and events, you become truly unstoppable! And of course, if you want to develop such system fast, you know what you need to do: contact us :) And we will take you on the fast lane so you get to have more visibility, more clients and bigger profits.

Another way to think about it...

As a Trainer, you deliver your 'content' to a number of people that gather in a room. There might be 10, 100, 1000 or more participants. But this approach requires your presence in the room, as well as constant marketing to fill up the audience. How about creating a webinar? You could reach people not within your geographical proximity. If you record your presentations or webinars, you could also sell them as products online. The beauty of this is that you make money while you sleep. That same content can bring 10 or 100 or 1000 times more money if you package it differently and sell it online.

TAKE ACTION NOW!

Write down 5 ideas you can implement to Repackage or Repurpose your product:

1. _____
_____
_____

2. _____
_____
_____

3. _____
_____
_____

4. _____
_____
_____

5. _____
_____
_____

Take that Giant Leap

Leverage with Technology

Nowadays, Technology is ubiquitous in business. It permeates every aspect of a business and streamlines everything from production and logistics to scheduling and advertising. Keeping up with the rapid advances and changes in Technology is a must, should your business have any hope of keeping up with the market. Any unused technological aid is a potential revenue stream dried up, either through wasteful management or production or simply through missed avenues of reaching customers.

Technology is not something I grew up with, and I don't grasp it as easily as the new generation. But when I saw its power, I became a fan.

> *Use Technology to make 10 or 100 times more with little or no effort! Automate your processes.*

See it in action!

When we started Tooliers®, we were sending emails using Mailchimp (software that distributes your newsletter and messages via email). We were sending campaigns, and we could see who opened our email, who clicked, who unsubscribed, and so on. They have some clever reports, and I was satisfied with their Solution. I wasn't looking for an alternative. Then a contact insisted I take a look at Infusionsoft, which takes things a step further and allows you to Automate marketing messages; i.e. the customer receives a series of emails when you want them to be sent, but without you having to do anything other than the initial programming (email #1 to be sent out within an hour of customer's first contact, email #2 a day later, email #3 a week later, and so on.) Compare this to a newsletter: you send it now and that's it. If a customer signs up tomorrow, they miss the newsletter I just sent.

The great thing with Automating emails is that you squeeze all opportunities to transform a potential lead into a customer and to push Sales to existing customers. **So now we are not creating campaigns – we are creating Marketing Automation.** We use campaigns, but once a campaign is created it is used for any new potential that comes into our Sales Funnel. With this Technology, we have Automated leads coming in and clients receive automatic campaigns based on their behavior, as well as Automated calls to action which they can take to buy online. This is making money while you sleep. Once created, such an asset generates money non-stop, no matter what you do and where you are.

I urge you to seek out the Technologies that can help you, and to apply them. Why do something manually that can be done automatically? Why leave money on the table by not doing things that Technology can do for you?

Why pay people to do what technology can do?

TAKE ACTION NOW!

Write down 5 Technology ideas or 5 problems you need to solve with Technology that you will research on Google to help your type of business:

1. _____
   _____
   _____

2. _____
   _____
   _____

3. _____
   _____
   _____

4. _____
   _____
   _____

5. _____
   _____
   _____

The best use of technology for us so far has been to attract clients online – on autopilot. You need to build your own online sales funnel (a sophisticated marketing system that generates business online on autopilot). Once it is built, clients will come to you with no more effort on your part.

Go to **www.ozanagiusca.com/sales-funnel-blueprint** and grab your Effective Sales Funnel Blueprint, to get started.

Tactic #101

Constantly Look for New Ideas

New Ideas should be the lifeblood of your business. They help you avoid becoming stale and keep you relevant, by giving you options for branching out and diversifying.

> **Add looking for New Ideas into your daily routine**
> **Train your team to include it in their schedule too**

Contemplate New Perspectives designed to improve your business. A New Perspective is another way of seeing things, issues, people; it is that different route to get home, or that New Voice you bring into your company. (See Tactic #91 'Bring New Voices into Your Company'.)

Engage in a New Passion that might have as an end result the improvement of your business. New Passion is doing what the company does, in a new way, as best as it can.

Engage in New Experiments designed to improve your business. New experiments are new actions, questions or tactics that generate New Ideas, that lead to Innovation.

> **Be open to everything around you**

Ask yourself New Questions (ones that have never been asked before in your company), such as:

- If you were going to create another industry, what would it be? Examples of new industries created by companies include: Microsoft – operating systems, Facebook – social networks, Google – internet search and advertising.

- If you were to start your business today from scratch and maximize

your impact, leverage and profitability, what would you do? What would your business look like?
- Think about your current reality and ask yourself 'What if?' questions.
- Think about the future and ask yourself 'What if?' questions.
- What Distribution Channels are you not using, or via which are Sales not being maximized?
- What Technology are you not using? What process have you not Automated?
- What are the trends in the market? Identify changes in the market as early as they appear, and figure out where the market is going.
- What massively improves the lives of your customers? What would wow your customer?

**Anyone can bring a great New Idea.
You never know where it comes from.
So be ready!**

I spend an hour per day...

> ... gathering New Ideas. I either read a blog post, watch a short video, or simply open emails from our competitors and people I respect and trust (yes, I have signed up to a few email distribution lists), and see what they do. I also go to seminars and conferences, and I meet other like-minded people and exchange view-points, what we have done, what we have learned or tried... and I often get ideas from these efforts that I can implement in my business. I either get ideas for marketing (oh, yes, this is a never-know-it-all subject, as things emerge constantly), or for other products. And most importantly, I speak to our customers, as they are the best source for further developments and improvements.

I challenge you to come up with one killer idea, or many improvements to what you are currently doing. That giant leap can be achieved by bringing to the market a wow product, or by making a series of improvements to your business that have a compound effect.

TAKE ACTION NOW!

Write down 5 directions you will consider for generating New Ideas. You might read a new book, or speak to someone in particular, or visit a new street in your neighborhood each day… or join my Smart Business Accelerator™ *(www.ozanagiusca.com/kim-en)*, where you don't just get ideas, you get ACTIONABLE ideas :)

1. _____
   _____
   _____

2. _____
   _____
   _____

3. _____
   _____
   _____

4. _____
   _____
   _____

5. _____
   _____
   _____

Smart Business System™

In my experience, which includes being responsible for increasing the profits of 100 companies over the past three years – in some cases doubling and even tripling profits – I've noticed that most people running a small business or working alone, face 7 main challenges to increasing sales.

Many believe their lack of further success is due to legislation, taxation, red tape, banks not lending or the government not helping small businesses, but the truth is there are 7 challenges that are within your control to overcome, which makes all the difference.

It is important to understand these challenges, to identify which ones you are facing and then to use the very best system to overcome your specific challenges.

Because I also faced these challenges, specifically when I was struggling to sell with Tooliers *(www.tooliers.com)*, I have developed the **Smarter Business System™**, which is our battle-tested solution for achieving objectives faster.

My team and I have been using this system on a daily basis. Initially we kept it for ourselves and for a select group of clients. Now, we share it freely with fellow entrepreneurs, experts and driven professionals who want more.

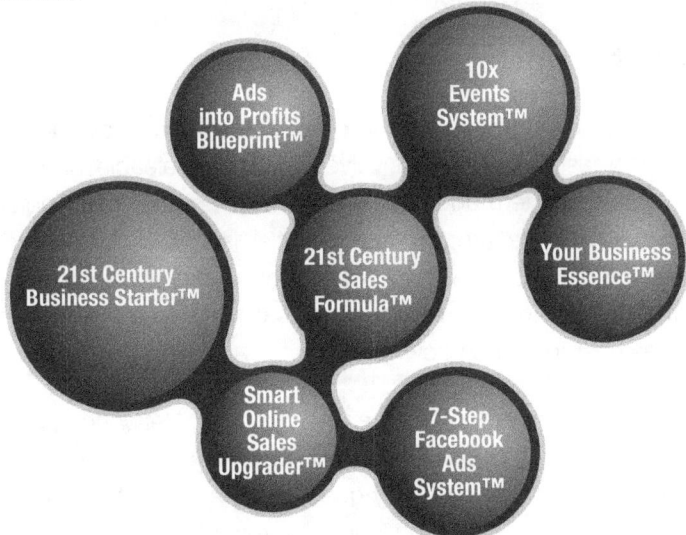

It is my pleasure to invite you to my online or live Master Classes in which I detail the system and its components.

Join me wherever it is convenient for you. Select from the events listed at **www.ozanagiusca.com/my-events** whatever best suits you and your needs. Some events are free and some require an investment.

Below I share more about the 7 challenges that block the growth of most businesses as well as the sub-system I have developed to overcome each challenge.

Challenge #1

Small business owners **want to sell more and have a stable, solid income**. Increasing the sales involves having a saleable product or service, a sales system and a way to feed this system with potential leads. Because there are various potential issues that need to be addressed before a business really takes off and grows exponentially, the **cash flow of most entrepreneurs is often like a rollercoaster** (sometimes up, more often down).

Too many meetings end up being a waste of time. Networking may be okay for social reasons, but few people buy from those they meet at events. A potential client suddenly goes cold... and whatever we do, it seems that people are simply no longer interested in buying.

Today, **people don't buy the way they used to**.

Due to the technology developments and the internet, the way people buy has changed. Which means that if you want to sell more, you also need to change your approach.

You need to adapt your business to the current reality. This is having the 21st Century Business Approach, the 21st Century Business Marketing Methods, and the 21st Century Business Essentials (this is not about the essentials in your business, which I am sure you have, but about the essentials that your business needs to give to you, its owner), because business as usual, as in the past, is no longer an option.

The key words here are Customer's Journey, a term that many experts talk about, but which is not understood and leveraged as it should be. This is about you **building a number of pre-programmed interactions with your potential clients, so you take them from "I don't know you" to buying from you and even recommending you to others**.

In most cases, such a 'journey' doesn't happen naturally. You need to engineer it, so your potential clients take the right steps (depending on where they are in relation to wanting your type of product or service) towards you and only you.

In order to build the road for such a journey, you need the 21st Century Business MAP.

21st Century Business MAP™

Smart Business System™

Deploying this system is the way to not only stay in business long term, but to thrive and generate increasing cash flow.

We are talking about combining online with offline activities, about talking to the potential client more but mainly in an automated or semi-automated manner, so you really leverage what you have and know so you achieve smarter profits faster.

I discuss this new approach and how to position your company, product or service and how to build your Customers' Journeys during the Smart Business Accelerator™ *(www.ozanagiusca.com/kim-en)*, strategic workshop over two days.

If you want to be in full control of your business; if you are fed up with trying various approaches which waste your money and time only to bring stress and frustration; and if you are committed now to investing to transform and scale your business, to maximize your profits and increase your impact so you achieve YOUR objectives, then I'm here to support you!

I invite you to join me for my next workshop where we will plan your Smarter Business *(www.ozanagiusca.com/kim-en)*.

Challenge #2

Before they started working with us, our clients were doing various activities, trying to sell to as many people as possible, but only getting a few clients.

I often see entrepreneurs busily developing a new product, serving existing clients, trying to source extra help, doing the admin tasks and even taking the trash out. They are constantly busy, feeling overwhelmed by how much they have to do… but what progress do they actually make?

For these entrepreneurs, I have developed the **Smart Online Sales Upgrader™**, to enable you to get more and better clients fast. Because generating business online can be done on auto or semi-auto pilot and when the system is deployed correctly, you have more time to do what you really love.

See in the illustration below how you can deploy this method to build your own system, to generate business online and have a constant and predictable cash flow.

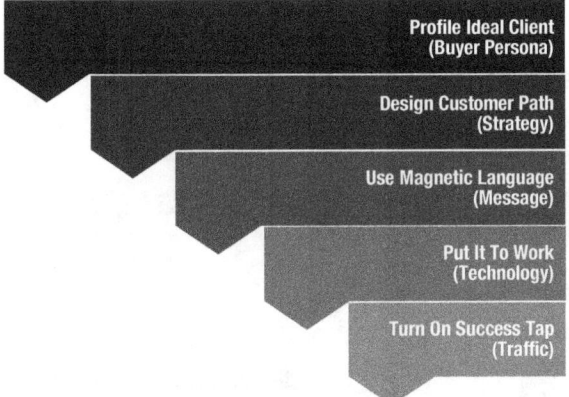

Under our guidance, participants in our Smart Online Sales Bootcamp™ *(www.ozanagiusca.com/sos-bootcamp-en)* achieve in two days what they have struggled to do on their own for years!

This method works because it has been tested on more than 400 entrepreneurs in most industries, ranging from professional services (consultants, coaches, experts) to manufacturing and retail.

The secret here is CLARITY. And to get clarity you need to go through a series of questions and, of course, answer them systematically, on paper.

Challenge #3

The majority of small businesses want more traffic in their store (online or offline) or visiting their website. Traffic is expensive, though, and they can't afford to waste resources on promotional activities that don't lead to sales.

We've figured that Facebook is the best platform right now to get traffic. It works for all businesses, but only when deployed correctly. If you are wondering if Facebook Ads are for you (i.e. investing in promotion on Facebook), join my next online Master Class *(www.ozanagiusca.com/facebook-ads-why-en)* on this subject.

Smart Business System™

We have developed the 7-Step Smart Business Facebook Ads System which we'll present during this Master Class. Simply go to **www.ozanagiusca.com/facebook-ads-system-en**, register, attend, take notes and implement.

We tested and tested… invested $100,000+ in our own campaigns and helped 300+ clients run profitable ads campaigns.

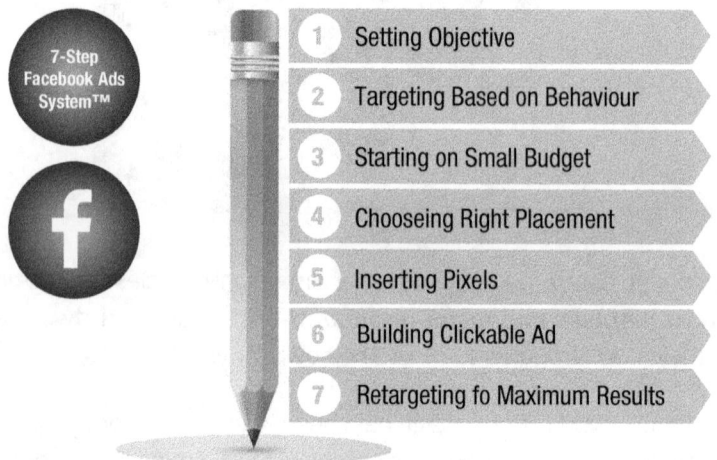

Challenge #4

Many people running their own show, be it a one-man venture or an established business, **need to sell but don't know how**. The truth is that selling is a skill you can learn. What's interesting is that most of our clients don't want to even consider taking sales courses. Because, just as they don't like others trying to sell to them, they know their potential clients don't want to hear from another pushy sales person. Besides, we set up our businesses based on our passion, because we want to help others and change the world, and we don't want to sound like second-hand car salesmen!

Many of my clients find themselves in a catch 22: they know their product or service is excellent but clients only realize and appreciate the value once they've experienced the product. Unable to clearly explain this amazing value to their potential clients, they have to constantly decrease their price just to make a sale.

The solution is the **21st Century Sales Formula™**, which is about helping your potential clients in advance so you show them, before asking for the sale, that you are the right person to help them.

The secret is to do it in such a way that you **create interest for your product or service so you don't even have to "sell" for a sale to happen**.

Imagine your best clients coming to you and begging you to sell to them!

Join my next Master Class on How to Accelerate Your Sales **(www.ozanagiusca.com/accelerate-sales)** to discover how easy this is. And yes, this is exactly what I do – I create interest and earn the trust of potential clients (like you) by offering real help in my Master Classes without any sales talk.

The more value you create in your marketplace, the more offers you can make. And of course, the more offers you make, the more sales you can achieve.

21st Century Sales Formula™

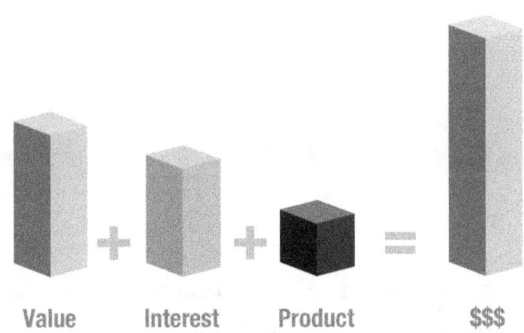

Value   Interest   Product $$$

Challenge #5

Most people in business have invested money, time and a lot of efforts in promotion, but the results are far from satisfying. This is because many tactics have been used in isolation without a strategy to back them up.

If you feel you have this challenge, then I highly encourage you to discover my Ads into Profit Blueprint™, where you can get answers to your burning questions about advertising, and more importantly, where you can ask more questions to help you get the RIGHT answers. Yes, it is only when you ask yourself the right questions that you can get helpful answers, so you can really get a good return on their promo budget.

Access Ads into Profits Master Class *(www.ozanagiusca.com/turn-ads-into-profitable-customers)* to get the right answers to the right questions.

Most entrepreneurs gain business in the traditional way. What you'll understand is how to expand beyond what you do well and break through the current sales figure, by adding other products, services, actions.

Traditional

- Website
- SEO
- Blog
- Social Media
- Refferals
- Meetings
- Networking
- Partnership
- Purchase lists
- Exhibition

For best results

- Customer's journey
- Online advertising
- Min 2 products
- Subscribers list
- Long term relationship

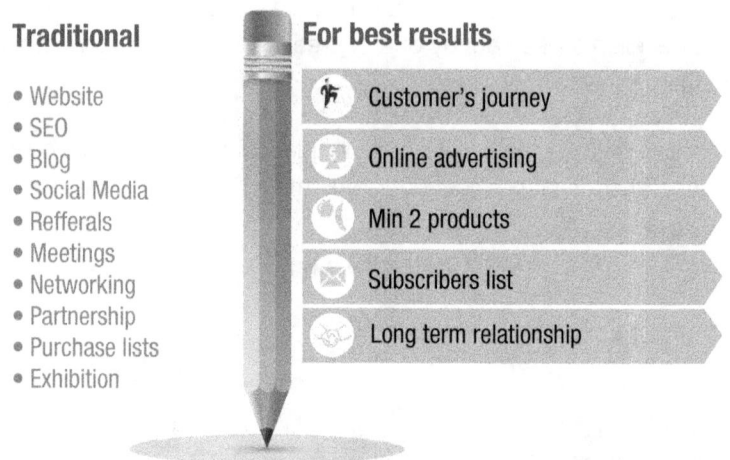

Challenge #6

Most people in business have a lot to do and not enough time to do it! They wish the working day had 48 hours so they could hold more meetings with potential clients and show their product to more people; to ultimately increase their sales and profits.

Well, there is a way for you to have 50 to 500 sales conversations in an hour or so. If you're asking yourself how this is possible, the **10x Events System™** *(www.ozanagiusca.com/10x-sales-bootcamp-en)* is for you.

Instead of giving away valuable information about your product or service during a sales conversation, share it in an educational or fun context, when your potential clients WANT to hear you talk about your offering.

The benefit of selling at events is that it is the most efficient way to sell, while getting your potential clients to love you for the experience and information you provide.

What do I mean by 'events'? It could be a workshop, a webinar, a series of online videos, a sampling / tasting or networking event, even a fashion show.

As you become closer to being an important player in your niche, you need to consider selling from the stage/ via events. This is not just for experts and trainers. Our clients who have introduced events in their marketing and selling activities include fashion, car repair, consultants, kids development, agricultural equipment, even doctors.

Of course, we are not talking about just any event! There is a way to hold events of the highest quality, which I share with you in the **10x Events System**™ *(www.ozanagiusca.com/10x-sales-bootcamp-en)*.

Challenge #7

Whether an established business or a newcomer, we all want to make more money. For some, money is a means to living the desired lifestyle, and for others it's a means to show they've achieved a lot and gained the appreciation and respect they deserve.

The challenges are that due to daily activities, and fires that need to be put out, entrepreneurs forget about their destination and most often behave as if lost in a dark forest.

In addition, in a world with so many people trying to sell so much it is difficult to grab your clients' attention. In a world where it is hard to get the right employees, and where communication is so important... it is not easy to 'construct' the right messages that attract the right people. You need to formulate your messages, with a view to ensuring that they are short and to the point, but most importantly, that they get to the heart of your potential clients. Such communication depends on the clarity you have about yourself and your business, and the connection between the two.

Smart Business System™

Unless you have a set of key messages that you and your team consistently use, you are just another seller, talking in generic terms like most people. This means you are forced to keep your price to a minimum, rather than getting paid for the real value you provide.

In other words, you need to carefully draft your key messages to use as your introduction, as a conversation opener or even on stage when you speak in front of more people. In order to get it right, you need to go to the essence of your business.

This is YOUR job!

No external consultants can come up with your key messages because they have to represent you. And the good news is that when you work on identifying such messages, you'll reconnect with your business and fall in love with it all over again.

The outcome is the right foundation for your communication, and you'll really become unstoppable and truly fulfilled when you answer the 7 WHY-based questions shown in the illustration below.

Big companies spent tens of thousands of dollars to identify their key messages. We've created a process to help you distill your key messages without spending an arm and a leg.

Would you like to overcome any of these challenges?

Then I invite you to join my **Smart Business Accelerator™** *(www.ozanagiusca.com/kim-en)* to discover how to build your Smarter Business, your business anchored in the current reality, and adapted to your current needs, aligned to your heart, so you feel in control and get to your destination faster.

Let's spend two days together, and you will

- Evaluate your growth opportunities to unleash the full potential of your business

- Eliminate time wasters, so you really focus on what is most important for you

Leave this workshop with clarity, ways to upgrade your business and a plan of action so you achieve your objectives faster.

Bonus: Love Letter

More value to you

I write about giving more Value than anticipated to your clients, about amazing your customers, about giving something for free. Here, it is my freebie to wow you.

Following, you will find the easieast way to come up with your marketing strategy. I give you the tool so you define your marketing strategy in 30 minutes. The tool is in the form of a letter you write to yourself as if it was written by your Best Customer. I call it 'Love Letter' because it shows the love your customers have to your company. It looks like a testimonial, but it is much more than that. Fill in the blanks. The point of this letter is to help you really understand your business, and what matters for your business's success. It looks like a testimonial, but it is way more than that. Once this letter sounds right, you know the recipe for your business's success. You have more clarity about your own business. You just need to execute correctly (You can do that by applying the 101 tactics in this book).

Below you will find a template for your Love Letter, as well as the letter I wrote for Tooliers®. This helps me 'name' my Persona, the benefits of my product (both logical and emotional), the impact my product has on customers' lives, how to find our customers, what to use to find customers, what I want my customers journey to be, how to ask them to provide recommendations, and more.

This template is your Strategy in a nutshell! And yes, you can use this to get inspiration for what you want your (real) client testimonials to look like.

I challenge you to fill in the blanks for your business. If you want the original, so you don't have to type up the template, visit **www.ozanagiusca.com/love-letter/** and grab your copy for free.

Love Letter Template

Dear **[Company Name]**,

My name is **[Persona's name]** and I must tell you I love your **[product type]** and I feel compelled to tell you my story.

I am a **[business type / life or lifestyle role]** who **[problem / passion statement]**. Thing is, that **[impact of pain / passion to life]**.

But **[Product Name]** changed my life.

Whenever I **[do specific things with product]** it works exactly as promised. Not only do I **[specific benefits]** but it makes me feel **[strong emotional reaction]**.

I find I use the product in that way every **[time period: hour / day / week, etc.]**

It's as if you looked me in the eye and said, '**[Persona's name]**, I promise you **[value promise]**'.

What I didn't expect, and share with other **[why shares with]** by **[mean of 'sharing']** is that you made me feel **[emotion impact]**.

Your product has forever **[how life changed]**.

I first heard of your product while **[activity / place related to title or life role]**. I decided to learn if it was really meant for me, so **[how to get more info]** where you said **[key message promise]**, which spoke directly to me. To tell you the truth, at first I was skeptical. But then, when you provided **[activity to induce trust]** I knew you were the right company.

[Influencer] endorsing the product was also key.

Still, I felt **[primary concern / objection]**.

Finally, when **[final action]** I was ready to **[sign up / buy / try]**.

I couldn't wait to get going, so as soon as I could, I **[first product setup / interaction]** to get started, and very quickly tried the **[feature to realize promise]** which made me feel hopeful that I had made the right decision.

Love Letter Example

Dear Tooliers®,

My name is Elisabeth. I must tell you that I love your Marketing Lens™ Diagnosis and Growth Program and I feel compelled to tell you my story.

I am an accounting firm owner who needs more clients. Thing is, I'm not earning enough. But Marketing Lens™ has changed my life.

Whenever I think of investing in marketing activities, I use the Marketing Lens™ and it works exactly as promised. Not only do I discover free ways to attract clients, but it also makes me feel like I really master marketing as a whole. I find myself working on one action to grow my business every other day, for only 15 minutes per day. I started this just one month ago and I already see 10% more enquiries from potential clients.

It's as if you looked me in the eye and said, 'Elisabeth I promise that you will discover ways of getting more customers by yourself without spending a cent.'

What I didn't expect, and I share this with other accounting firm owners in our regular ACCA meetings, is that you made me feel like a great businessperson, not just an accountant. I truly *feel* I own my business now; I am not just a simple accountant who has a job in my own company.

Marketing Lens™ Diagnosis and Growth Program has forever changed how I market our accounting services.

I first heard of your product while browsing The American Institute of CPAs online. I decided to learn if it was really meant for me and I went to **www.tooliers.com**. You said that I would get answers to questions I had never asked myself and this really resonated with me. To tell you the truth, at first I was skeptical about getting actions tailored to my business and given automatically to me by a computer! No one knows my industry better than me. But then, when you provided the Marketing Lens™ Diagnostic Report I knew you were the right company. Your assessment of why I was not attracting the customers I wanted was spot on. You also showed me what I need to focus on attracting the customers I deserve.

Entrepreneur.com's endorsement of Marketing Lens™ Diagnosis and Growth Program was also key to my decision to check you out. They are a trusted resource with information for every business owner.

Still, even at this stage I felt marketing was too complicated for me. Besides, I truly love performing accounting services, *not* marketing my business. Finally, after having followed the Action Plan on Social Media, I was ready to buy the Marketing Lens™ Growth Program. I understand now that things are not as complicated as they seemed, and that even I can attract and engage online with potential clients for my firm!

I couldn't wait to get going, so as soon as I could, I performed the Marketing Lens™ Diagnosis. I quickly started with the first action on Sales Funnel Tactic, which made me feel comfortable that I'd made the right decision. I see how, by the end of the Growth Program, I will have become a marketing guru for my business; customers will come to us, as bees are attracted to a honeypot. And you know what? I now see myself as *managing an accounting practice*, and no longer as doing accounting services. The latter is the job of my employees!

> **Want to grow your business and don't know how and where to start?**

> **Or do you have a business challenge you want an expert opinion on?**

I love bringing new ideas to the table and contributing to the growth of any kind of business, from e-commerce sites to professional services providers; from retail to entertainment. Every industry has its own particularities, but all have one thing in common: **apply best business practices and your business will succeed.** It's exactly this subject that I've mastered, and I can help any business implement best practices, regardless of size, industry or geography.

So contact me via my website and I'll respond within 24 hours.

www.ozanagiusca.com

If you just want to stay in touch, connect with me on:

- www.facebook.com/giusca.ozana
- plus.google.com/+OzanaGiusca
- www.linkedin.com/in/ozanagiusca
- www.twitter.com/OzanaGiusca
- www.youtube.com/user/ozana197

Glossary of Terms

Glossary of Terms

These definitions are crafted to be as simple as possible, and are explained in the context of this book.

AAA rating - refers to the evaluation of credit worthiness; i.e how trustworthy a company is to do business with. The highest rating is AAA, descending to C (low) and D (even worse).

Action Plan or Fast Track implementation Plan - a step-by-step guide to work on and improve various areas of the business (strategy, sales, marketing, etc.) and sub-areas (educational marketing, writing blogs, building a website, email marketing etc.).

Affiliate Marketing - this is an agreement whereby a business rewards someone (affiliate person or company) for each visitor / customer brought by the affiliate's own marketing efforts, or for each purchase generated by the affiliate, within a time frame.

Attractive Premium - an item included in a pack, together with less interesting items, and sold as a bundle. It's a good way of moving slow-selling products.

Automate / Automating / Automation - using software rather than employees to undertake automatically some processes within the company.

Business-to-business (B2B) - a business that sells to other businesses. Compare with Business-to-Consumer (B2C), which is when the company sells to consumers / individuals.

Better Offer - a product (service) or a bundle of products (services), designed to offer more value (than usual) for the same dollar spent.

Brand - the name, design, symbol, colors or any other feature that identifies one company or product. For example, Coca-Cola is one brand, Fanta is another; they both belong to The Coca-Cola Company.

Branding via Association - linking the brand of one business with a better known brand, so the lesser known brand 'borrows' from the popularity of the other.

Business Doctor - business growth solution consisting of (i) diagnosing a business (see Business Lens®), (ii) designing a customized action plan to optimize and grow the company and (iii) implementing that plan.

Business Lens® - company assessment toolkit to show business owners the naked truth about their company. It identifies unexploited growth potential. It covers everything that matters for the growth of the business (analyzes in detail 15 business dimensions, including Strategy, Innovation, Leadership, Superstar Organization, Marketing, Sales, Human Resources, Motivation, Support Systems, Follow-Up and Organizational Culture) a Tooliers® service.

Business Lens® Diagnostic - the process of answering multiple choice questions and getting a business evaluation report that shows what the business does well and what it needs to focus on a Tooliers® service.

Buying Criteria - the requirements and rules that one buyer uses to buy a product, such as quality, price, availability, reliability, durability, comfort, habit, safety, freshness, coolness, taste, production methods, etc.

Chunking - grouping together information into ideally sized pieces, so they can be used effectively to produce the outcome one wants without stress or shutdown.

Chunk Down - dealing with smaller parts of information / activities in order to understand or do them effectively. Especially useful when the information / activities are new or complex.

Chunk Up - dealing with larger parts of information / activities in order to understand / accomplish more at once. Especially useful when one faces known information or deals with routine activities

Complementary Product (Service) - product (service) whose use is interrelated with the use of another product (service); e.g. cartridges and printers are complementary products.

Cross Selling - one business selling its product (service) to another business's customers, and vice versa.

Distribution Channel - the path through which products travel from vendors to consumers; e.g. coffee travels from farmer to exporter, to importer, to distributor, and to the retailer who sells to the end user.

Educational Marketing - sharing valuable information with potential customers, for their benefit and to build trust.

Gift with Purchase - providing another product (service) when someone buys a certain product (service); e.g. a sample cream when you buy a perfume.

Host-Parasite Relationship - adding one's product to be sold passively together with another product that is marketed and sold by the other business (the 'parasite' company doesn't do anything to make sales happen). E.g. producer of a dress adds belt from another manufacturer, and promotes and sells the dress with the belt.

Inducement(s) - an incentive to make the offering more appealing to the customer, and the sale sweeter.

Joined Offers - offering one's product together with another product; both parties promote the combined offer.

Joint Venture (JV) - business agreement for a set period, in which each party undertakes some efforts, for the benefit of all parties.

Lead - term used for a potential customer in the first stage of a sales process; i.e. the business made the initial contact with that prospect, be it (directly or indirectly) via the business's website, or via a phone call or meeting.

Lead Nurturing Email - email designed to build relationships and trust with prospective customers in a consistent and relevant manner.

Limited Edition - the manufacturing of a product in a limited quantity, to make it a more interesting purchase for the buyer.

Limited Time Offer - an offer that has a specific deadline, to give potential buyers a clear reason to act without delay.

Limited Stock Offer - a limited number of items made available, to give potential buyers a clear reason to act without delay.

Locking Sales In - securing long-term sales; e.g. signing a long-term contract or ensuring customer comes back for repeat purchase.

Offer Email - an email to promote a product, to ask for a purchase.

Potentials or Prospects - potential customers.

Pre-emptive Anti-competition Strategy - a strategy employed by one business to lead potentials to only consider its offering, thus blocking its competitors even before they are considered by the buyer as potential sellers.

Risk Reversal - marketing strategy based on removing the risks of the buyer to help them make the purchase decision; e.g. 30-day money back guarantee.

ROI (Return on Investment) - a performance measure calculated as the benefit produced by an investment divided by the cost of that investment (expressed as %); commonly used to evaluate the efficiency of an investment or to compare different real or potential investments.

Glossary of Terms

ROTI (Return on Time Invested) - the return on the time invested into an activity or project (valued in dollar amount per hour).

Sales Funnel - a metaphoric description of the sales process from initial contact to final sale. It is called a 'funnel', because there are many leads (cold potentials), and as one gets closer to the sale, the number decreases.

Soft Skills - a cluster of personality traits, social abilities, communication, language, and personal habits that characterize relationships of one person with others.

Tooliers® - online platform with business growth tools designed to help small and mid-sized business owners to take their companies to the next level. Founded by Ozana Gusca.

Ultimate Strategic Position (USP) (not to be confused with Unique Selling Proposition) – the final perception that a company wants to have in the eyes of the customer.

Unique Value Proposition (UVP) - a few words used by one business to tell prospective customers why they should buy their product or use their service; it tells how this business adds more value or better solves a problem than competing businesses (similar to Unique Selling Proposition).

Value Papers - promotional materials (such as flyers, leaflets, brochures, catalogues) that give, besides the usual information / advertising content, monetary value to the holder towards the purchase of the product / service being promoted (such as % discount, $ reduction, gift); the goal is to incentivize a sale.

> 'Any ending is a new beginning.'
> Ozana Giusca

Make the most of the knowledge you have received or gotten from this book and take your business to the next level.

In this series

Attract More Customers
Vol. 1

More for You, the Leader
Vol. 2

Increase Internal Efficiency
Vol. 3

Get the Most out of Your Team
Vol. 4

More for You, the Leader
Vol. 5

Sustain Your Business Long-Term
Vol. 6

Take that Giant Leap
Vol. 7

www.ozanagiusca.com/BusinessUnlimited

www.ingramcontent.com/pod-product-compliance
Lightning Source LLC
Chambersburg PA
CBHW070259230526
45470CB00002B/650